SPIRIT OF STOKE MANDEVILLE

The Story of Sir Ludwig Guttmann

SPIRIT OF STOKE MANDEVILLE

The Story of
Sir Ludwig Guttmann

SUSAN GOODMAN

With a Foreword by
HRH The Prince of Wales

COLLINS
8 Grafton Street, London W1
1986

William Collins Sons and Co Ltd
London · Glasgow · Sydney · Auckland
Toronto · Johannesburg

Those who were close to Ludwig Guttmann and who knew his background intimately urged him to write his memoirs. He had, they believed, a unique version of recent history to tell, both from the medical and political viewpoint. He had, as he recorded with feeling, 'experienced the depths to which mankind can sink, having witnessed the terrible effects of Nazism ... as well as the forces of courage and justice which humanity can marshal to defeat intolerance and cruelty'. He had worked with men he termed 'giants' in his own speciality of medical and surgical neurology. With the enthusiasm he brought to all his undertakings, Guttmann started to write.

Given permission and encouragement by his family, in recounting this story I have, where possible, included Ludwig Guttmann's own words.   S.G.

Goodman, Susan
Sir Ludwig Guttmann: spirit of Stoke Mandeville.
1. Guttmann, Sir Ludwig   2. Paraplegia——Great
Britain——Biography
I. Title
362.4'3'0924   RC406.P3

ISBN 0 00 217341 7

First published 1986
© Susan Goodman 1986

Phototypeset in Monophoto Garamond by
Butler & Tanner Ltd, Frome and London
Made and Printed in Great Britain by
William Collins Sons and Co Ltd, Glasgow

CONTENTS

ILLUSTRATIONS

Throwing the discus.

Putting the shot.

Joan Scruton, Ludwig Guttmann and Charlie Atkinson, known at Stoke Mandeville as The Three Musketeers.

Sir Ludwig and Lady Guttmann with their eldest grand-daughter, Clare.

HRH the Princess of Wales after opening the 1985 International Stoke Mandeville Games.

KENSINGTON PALACE

It is amazing to think that not so many years ago the treatment of paraplegics was generally regarded as a waste of time. In those days some eighty per cent of people who sustained spinal cord injuries were dead within three years. Today their life expectancy is normal.

For this we owe much to Sir Ludwig Guttmann, who revolutionised the treatment and care of paraplegics and tetraplegics by making it possible for such people to live active lives in wheelchairs, when previously their days were spent semi-recumbent.

His work at Stoke Mandeville Hospital rapidly reached all corners of the world when the International Stoke Mandeville Games and the first Olympics for people in wheelchairs were established. He enjoyed a particularly close relationship with his patients — those 'hopeless' cases whom no one else cared to treat in the early days of the war. He pioneered methods of looking after disabled people which helped towards the current thinking that people with spinal injuries should live as part of — and not apart from — the community.

Sir Ludwig made many significant discoveries through his research and his contribution as a scientist was recognised by his election as a Fellow of the Royal Society.

A small, dynamic man, he inspired intense loyalty in all

9

members of his team. He identified himself totally with the welfare of paralysed people and any attack on his various organisations was considered treason! No battle on behalf of his patients was too small to excite his complete interest and dedication. He was a man of genius and his personal warmth and humour were infectious.

Over the years I have admired his work and it was with particular pleasure that I became a Patron of the British Paraplegic Sports Society, and attended the great man's eightieth birthday party.

Throughout the world people will have their personal memories and anecdotes of Sir Ludwig. I am delighted that Susan Goodman has produced this biography of such a remarkable person, whose inspiration continues to bring new hope to many who have had their lives shattered by spinal lesions.

1939

AFTER YEARS of increasing persecution under the Nazi regime in Germany, Ludwig Guttmann, a distinguished neurologist and neurosurgeon, his wife and their two small children, were at last granted exit visas. Their emigration from Germany came about through the efforts of the British Society for the Protection of Science and Learning, with whom Guttmann had secretly been in touch. The family would be allowed to bring some clothes, a few personal effects and a total of forty marks with which to start their new life.

They finally reached Dover on 14 March 1939. It was one of those uninviting days common to the early English spring – bitterly cold, with rain and sleet showers and blowing a gale. As they queued in a draughty shed, part of a long line of anxious immigrants, Dr Guttmann witnessed a simple and quite ordinary act of human kindness. After living for years under the strain of the Nazi regime – the violence of Kristallnacht, the ever-present threat of the Gestapo at the door, seeing the condition of men released from concentration camps – it moved Else and Ludwig Guttmann to tears, and it was this incident which symbolised for them the common human decency which they had watched vanish in their own country:

'The immigration officer came in with a grim and

11

unfriendly countenance. He watched the sad faces of the immigrants – almost penniless, family, friends and possessions abandoned in another country. But he was unmoved, he had seen it all before. Then, as his gaze wandered along the queue from the dais, his facial expression suddenly changed and in a friendly voice he called out: "Who are those little children there at the back?" When I signalled that they were ours, his immediate response was: "Will you please come first, children shouldn't stay in a draught." After all our tribulations, this sign of humanity really stunned us. Else wept and I got a constriction in my throat. This was England!'

It was also the start of a remarkable story, of one man's fight to bring hope and the chance of a useful life to spinally injured men and women. Before that story could begin, however, another, just as remarkable, was enacted in Europe in the first forty years of this century. What follows is the story of Ludwig Guttmann's life, the times through which he lived, and his dynamic achievements.

Silesia,
1899-1917

LUDWIG GUTTMANN was born on 3 July 1899 in the small German township of Tost, Upper Silesia. It was the time 'when Queen Victoria was still at the helm of the British Empire and her son, Edward, an elderly Crown Prince. Her grandson, Kaiser Wilhelm II – son of Kaiser Frederick III and of Vicky, her beloved daughter – was my monarch.'

Ludwig was the eldest child and only son of Bernhard and Dorothea Guttmann; three sisters followed. The family was Jewish. The father was 'a quiet, upright and hard-working man. He was a distiller by profession, owning his own business and gaining a good reputation in his trade, even beyond the district in which we lived, by introducing special brands of liquor. Through hard work – he began work at seven in the morning – and against tough competition, he developed a prosperous business. He fought loyally with the German army in the First World War.' The mother was by all accounts a strong and much loved personality, with a keen sense of justice which her son inherited.

In 1902 the Guttmanns moved to Königshütte, a town some hundred miles from Breslau with a population of about seventy thousand, where they lived for more than twenty years. After the partition of Upper Silesia in 1921, Königshütte became Polish, first called Krulovskahuta and later renamed Chorzow. It was situated in the heart of the region's

13

heavy industrial zone, surrounded by coalmines and sustaining a huge iron foundry of several square miles, as well as smelting and blast furnace plants. Undoubtedly because of Königshütte's polluted atmosphere, Dorothea Guttmann suffered badly from catarrh. Her son Ludwig sometimes accompanied her to a spa in the nearby mountains and never forgot 'the spectacle of the gargle hall and the cacophonic noises made by patients taking the cure'.

As a boy, he had a happy home, indeed it seems to have been an idyllic childhood which furnished him for life with memories of walks through summer fields on his grandfather's farm, of rough-and-tumble companionship with his many cousins. In old age, seeing the film *Fiddler on the Roof*, he was vividly reminded of these roots, the years when he was growing up in a Jewish community in what was then German territory. It was the background experience which shaped his life.

In that part of East Central Europe, records of early Jewish settlements, probably refugees from the Crusades, can be traced back to the thirteenth century; earliest evidence of Jews in Breslau is a tombstone of 1203. Immigration from Germany in the thirteenth and fourteenth centuries increased the Jewish population, and over a period of several hundred years more than fifty Jewish communities were established in Silesia, the largest of them in Breslau. There were periodic expulsions and bouts of severe persecution. By 1700 there were still two hundred Jewish families in Silesia on whom, in 1713, the government levied a 'Toleranzstever' or Tolerance Tax, an idea resurrected to fierce purpose over two hundred years later by the Nazis.

Many of the Jewish settlers who survived had become proprietors of small country taverns. Thereafter, the expanding Jewish population of the region was divided between pedlars, small tradesmen and the privileged few who became wealthy through the area's industrial development. By the nineteenth and early twentieth centuries Silesian Jewry was taking an active part in the cultural and economic life of the country: although the pinnacle of professional life was denied them, the majority considered themselves, above all else, loyal German subjects. This was certainly true of Bernhard Guttman, who immediately joined the army in 1914 although he had reached his forty-fifth birthday, the upper age limit for service, five days after war had been declared. Jews could practise their religion in reasonable security, so it was into a relatively calm and favoured era of Silesian history that Ludwig Guttmann was born at the turn of the century. His nostalgic memories of childhood perfectly evoke the rural life-style of a simpler time:

'Both my parents came from farming stock with large families, ten children on my father's side and twelve on my mother's. My paternal grandfather, Joseph, a tall, rather taciturn man, developed the larger farm through hard work and good business sense. I remember accompanying him in later years on his trips to the horse market, and was impressed by his skill and toughness with which he dealt with the horse traders. There was no written contract when a horse was bought or sold: the two parties just touched each other with two fingers of their right hand to seal the bargain, and this agreement was never broken.

'My grandmother, Rose, was a small wiry woman; in addition to organising and governing the household of ten children and male and female servants with an iron hand, she was a herbalist of local fame. Whenever anyone in the surrounding villages had some ailment they would first consult "Rose", who had the great commonsense and insight to distinguish between mild ailments, which she "healed" with all kinds of herbs, and the more serious afflictions, when she would call in the family doctor from twenty miles away, who would arrive in his landau in any weather conditions.

'During school holidays my grandparents' house was filled with grandchildren, some of us somewhat unruly boys, and it was amazing how that little lady dealt with our high spirits. I remember how on one occasion, two cousins and I paid a visit to a relative in one of the neighbouring villages. The owner of an inn, for a joke, gave us too much wine, with the obvious effect on twelve-year-old boys. We found our way home but one of us, my cousin Bruno, who really had had "one over the eight", collapsed in my grandparents' garden. My Aunt Berthe, a widow with two children who lived with my grandparents, became hysterical and shouted for her mother to come quickly as Bruno was "dead". Rose, looking at the boy lying flat out, calmly diagnosed: "This little pig is drunk" and taking a pitcher of cold water, poured it over his head. With this emergency treatment both Bruno and Aunt Berthe quickly recovered, and Rose did not miss the opportunity to lecture us on the evils of drink!

'It was not unusual for ten or twelve grandchildren of various ages to be spending their summer holidays with Joseph and Rose, who had to employ a nanny to help look after the younger ones. One of my happiest memories is of accompanying my grandfather, after five o'clock morning prayers, through the fields of his farm. It was his custom to take a boy and a girl with him during these walks. Joseph, tie-less, wearing an old cap and smoking his first pipe of the day, with the then customary long stem, large bowl and lid, would point out the beauties of nature, knowing the name of every flower, crop and animal. The older grandchildren had to help during harvesting by taking food to the men and women foreign farm workers in the fields. They came in a group from villages beyond the Austrian border during corn harvesting. The grain in those days was not cut by machines, but still by scythe and sickle.

'Every Friday evening, when Sabbath began, my grand-parents would gather all the children around them before dinner for evening prayers after which every child received a sip of wine. Rose, seated on an old wooden trunk and wearing her best dress with a silken white bow, delivered blessings on us all. The ritual was repeated at the close of the Sabbath, Habdala, when it was the privilege of the youngest grandchild to hold aloft the lighted candle which, according to an old tale, was supposed to make the child grow tall. Alas – it did not work for me!

'My maternal grandfather, Markus Weissenberg, in addition to his farm also had a small contractor's business with the nearby coalmine. He was a small, rather studious type, often sitting for long hours studying the Bible and looking, with his large white beard, more like a Rabbi than a farmer. Although a devout Jew, he did not share that intolerance so often inherent in that section of Judaism, as in orthodox sections of other religions. When one of his own daughters, Aunt Johanna, fell in love with a Protestant, an administrative officer of a nearby coal mine, despite my grandmother Babette's protest he gave his blessing to their wedding. Many years later, I better understood the anguish of mind and spirit which gripped the play character, Tevye, when he had to choose between love for his daughter in her marriage to a Gentile and the dogma of orthodox Jewish belief – I was immediately reminded of Markus, Babette and Hanna. There could hardly ever have been a more harmonious marriage than that of Hanna and her husband, Reinhard Gotz. As a boy, I was often in their home as they also lived in Konigshutte; both remained faithful to their religions. Their real sorrow was that they would have to be buried in different cemeteries.

'Markus left most of the organisation of the family of twelve children to my grandmother, a forceful character, resolute and outspoken, with a keen moral sense – characteristics my mother inherited. On occasions, Babette could become short-tempered and would tolerate no nonsense. She employed for her young children a house teacher, whom she threw out one day when she discovered he had unfairly punished one of her daughters.

'One of Babette's annual performances was to pickle cabbage, Sauerkraut, in a large barrel. Layers of cut cabbage, salt, some caraway seeds and apples were carefully placed in the barrel, and when it was full it was covered with a piece of wood. Babette, having put on special, thick white stockings, to the delight of her grandchildren would then stamp ceremoniously on the wooden cover to press down the contents. The fluid resulting from this was scooped out and finally a heavy stone was laid onto the wooden cover and the cabbage and apples left to ferment. The liquid was removed daily and the end product was delicious. Babette became quite an outstanding personality in the village of Schwientochlowitz. When she died at the age of ninety-seven, in 1920 during the time of the referendum in Upper Silesia, many villagers paid their respects to her, Germans standing on one side of the road, Poles on the other as the carriage with her coffin passed down the High Street. Babette's brother, Ludwig Silberfeld, was also a rather tough character: when his son came to introduce his fiancee, not having previously asked his father's permission, Ludwig glowered at her and exclaimed: "I am damned if it is a pleasure!"'

Education in Silesia at that time was the exception rather than the rule and had to be paid for. But Bernhard Guttmann, as well as his parents and parents-in-law, determined that the new generation should have a better chance in life than they had had, and they were successful. Of the numerous grandchildren, three became teachers, three doctors, four lawyers, two musicians and the rest well-to-do businessmen.

Ludwig Guttmann looked back on his primary school education as a pleasant experience. At nine he entered high school, called a Humanist Gymnasium since the main subjects were Latin and Greek. Bernhard regarded education as a privilege, however, not merely a right, and expected his four children to work hard. Ludwig did not always please him in this respect. Although extremely intelligent and with wide interests, his personality was too strongly individual not to find the restraints of any school irksome. As he put it himself:

'With entry into High School my conflicts with the realities of the world began. I was not a model student, and although I did quite well in the three lower classes I became increasingly bored by the rigid routine and stuffy and petty attitude of some of my teachers, who had no sense of humour or understanding of the vulnerability of young souls. Some of them were odd characters, frozen in biased trains of thought and theories. There were exceptions, however, such as my history teacher, and history became my favourite subject, the only one in which I had continually good records; and it still fascinates me today. Another was the master of the school choir, which I joined, having a good soprano voice. One of the highlights of our choir was the performance of Haydn's *Creation* at a public concert. And I also became fond of our gymnastic teacher who, outside the lessons and during class excursions, abandoned the usual strict distance between teacher and pupil and stood with us on equal footing, rather uncommon in those days. It made him very popular amongst the class without losing respect.

19

'I had only one aim at school – never to repeat a year in the same class, which even as a boy I considered to be a lost year of life. I achieved this with some virtuosity. Three-quarters of the year I paid little attention to some of the subjects, being more interested in sport and the German Scout movement. Then my father would receive a letter from the school, always handed to him personally by the beadle, called Pedell, and after a serious talk on his part I would settle down to some hard work and succeed in scraping through. This procedure year after year earned me the nickname "Season Worker" by my teachers. I did a great deal of sport – running and football in particular – and my main interest was photography, the only subject in which I ever received an award at school.

'When I was eleven, I joined the "Pathfinder" Corps – the German equivalent of the Scout Movement in Britain, though with a slightly more military touch. I enjoyed all the field exercises including climbing, first aid and camping with the open fire cooking. My mother gave me some cookery lessons, including recipes which I more or less successfully served up to my comrades when I later became group leader. On one of our excursions in the neighbourhood of the Duke of Pless's hunting lodge, I saw Kaiser Wilhelm II leaving the lodge in the fancy hunting dress which was worn in those days, and I could not let such a rare opportunity pass without having a "shot" at my monarch – with my camera.'

Perhaps because it touched his acute sense of history, this memory in particular was one which remained absolutely clear to Guttmann all his life.

As a Jewish family, most of the religious rites and customs were observed in the Guttmann home, 'but without being fanatic'. The family attended synagogue regularly on Friday evenings and on all festivals. His sister Alice still remembers the devotion between her mother and Ludwig, the only son, and the strict moral authority which Dorothea exerted over him. But even as a boy of twelve, Guttmann's quick and highly original mind was troubled by the rigidity inherent in all religions when scrupulously practised:

'At that time there was an incident at school which made me question, for the first time, certain orthodox forms. The Jewish boys in my High School had to go to school on the Sabbath; but they were excused from writing and carrying school books which were therefore left at school on Friday, in keeping with the Jewish custom that one must not carry anything on the Sabbath ... we were not even allowed to switch on electric lights. Well, on one occasion, I was pulling my handkerchief out of my pocket to blow my nose when my friend Albrecht, the Rabbi's son, told me I had committed a sin by carrying a handkerchief in my pocket. When I enquired how *he* would blow *his* nose, he pointed to the handkerchief pinned to his braces thus, according to orthodox doctrine, making the handkerchief part of his wearing apparel. Indignantly I exclaimed: "But you are cheating the Good Lord!" When I later expressed my disbelief in this kind of religious bigotry to my mother, she was bewildered by my rebellion against such traditional forms or religion. Whilst, at this early age, I began to question the rationale of orthodox forms, I nevertheless remained loyal to the Jewish faith.'

At the age of thirteen, like all Jewish boys, he was confirmed in the synagogue. At his Bar Mitzvah he read a portion of the Law from the Scroll and was afterwards addressed by the Rabbi from the pulpit and blessed. 'So suddenly I was considered a man and a full member of the congregation!' His parents invited friends and relatives to an evening dinner-dance. Guttmann records:

'They dutifully turned up and I had to make my first after-dinner speech, which was prepared with the help of my

Hebrew teacher. I started off confidently: "Parents, Rabbi, relatives and friends," but there I stuck, and had to read the whole thing from the manuscript – to my mother's pride and my teacher's displeasure, as he had expected me to speak freely. Amongst the many presents I received was an Omega watch from my father, which I cherished throughout all the years until, alas, it was stolen during a burglary at our house in High Wycombe in 1969, together with many other sentimental treasures.

'Although I never personally experienced any religious intolerance during my schooldays, there was one occasion in the early years of my High School life when I was involved in an anti-semitic row. One of my Jewish friends, a rather timid chap, complained that another boy in our class had insulted him by calling him a "damned Jew". Taking up cudgels on his behalf I accosted the boy in question who, incidentally, was a good friend of mine, and asked for an explanation. By way of response he pulled my tie, of which I had been inordinately proud, it being my first tie and a gift from my mother. Naturally this started a fight, during which I knocked out one of his teeth. This incident occurred during the break, when all the boys, supervised by a teacher, were in the school playground and were now watching the fight. On this occasion the supervisor was our history teacher – a tall, distinguished-looking man, always meticulously dressed in his long frock-coat, a classical example of a Prussian Lieutenant of the Reserve – who stopped the fight on the ringing of the bell to resume lessons.

'The next lesson was history, and when the teacher learned the reason for the fight from somebody from the class I was reprimanded for having been too rough; but my opponent received an hour's detention for his anti-semitic conduct – a serious punishment which was recorded in the boy's half-yearly report. The boy's father, himself a teacher in a Catholic school, was so upset that he came to apologise for his son's misdemeanour to both the insulted boy's father and to my father.' That incident, apparently handled with good sense and justice on all sides, had an ominous postscript. Many years later, the boy who started the row in the playground became one of the leaders of the Nazified provincial lawyers' society in Silesia.

So, despite a certain scepticism, Ludwig Guttmann's roots were firmly planted in Jewish religious and cultural life. His family lived peaceably and relatively prosperously in and around Königshütte as Germans who happened to be of the Jewish faith. Emancipation for German Jews had been hard won. During the liberation war against Napoleonic France, Jews had fought as volunteers. As a direct result of the Stein-Hardenberg reform of the German constitution in 1812, they were granted full rights of citizenship even though they were, in practice, still debarred from certain professions. During the 1880s a storm of anti-semitism sent shock waves through German universities. A prime instigator of this was Stocker, the court chaplain of Kaiser Wilhelm II: 'At that time, the *Venia Legende*, or permission to teach, of university professors could be summarily withdrawn. This happened to Ludwig Edinger, a Jew, who was Privat Dozent, honorary lecturer, at the medical faculty of Giessen University. Edinger later founded the Neurological Institute in Frankfurt, and the university there elected him Professor Ordinarius in Neurology. His Institute became a magnet for distinguished scientists from many countries, including the outstanding British neurologist, Gordon Holmes. Dr Holmes told me that Edinger offered him a university Assistantship which he reluctantly declined as the post demanded, he said, his acceptance of German citizenship, which he could not undertake.'

Another area of professional life in which Jews were severely limited was the army. Like any other male German citizen, a Jew was required to do military National Service, but no matter what a man's abilities or ambitions, if he was a Jew he was virtually excluded from becoming a regular officer. Jews were even excluded from becoming officers of the Reserve, with certain rare exceptions like war-time emergencies. This embargo was largely due to the deep-seated anti-semitic attitude of the German Army Corps and their exclusive power to elect officers.

There was undoubtedly some underlying concern, for in 1891 the League for Defence Against Anti-Semitism was founded on the initiative of non-Jewish politicians, scientists and economists, followed in 1893 by the foundation of the Central Association of German Citizens of Jewish Faith, known as CV from the German Central Verein Deutscher Staatsburger Judischen Glauben and in 1896 by the Association of German Students of Jewish Faith, otherwise KC, from Kartell-Convent Deutscher Studenten Judischen Glauben. There were also other Jewish students' associations and a few inter-denominational student fraternities. It was the CV group that became the principal organisation of German Jewry.

At the end of the nineteenth century and the beginning of the twentieth, Jews in Russia and Poland were subjected to brutal waves of pogroms, resulting in increasing emigration of Jews to Germany and other Western countries. A child at the time, Guttmann clearly remembered a young Polish couple staying at his parents' house in Konigshutte, fleeing Poland and in transit to the United States. Some emigrants were granted permission to stay in Germany but the majority used the country as a way-station. Help was given to them principally by the Aid Association of German Jews, but many individuals and other charitable organisations gave financial assistance and practical advice on resettlement. The Aid Association of German Jews also set up and financed the first technical school in Haifa for the benefit of early Jewish immigrants in Palestine. Guttmann believed that these facets of German Jewish life, as well as the growth of Zionism in Germany, were insufficiently recognised 'in view of the prejudices to which German Jews were exposed as a whole by fellow Jews in the UK and other countries' when they became refugees from Nazi persecution.

At the beginning of the First World War, Kaiser Wilhelm II issued a manifesto proclaiming the equality of all German citizens, regardless of faith or conviction, but even then only a small number of Jews were commissioned as junior officers in the Reserve. This attitude continued even during the period of the Weimar Republic when German Jews felt quite secure in their civil rights in accordance with the constitution, considering themselves first and foremost German nationals. Like Jews in England, the United States and elsewhere, they lived as full citizens; they took part in, and contributed to, the political, economic, cultural and social life of the country. Although it is not always widely recognised, Jews in Germany, both as individuals and through national organisations, continuously fought against racial intolerance and stood up for human and civil rights.

In August 1914 Great Britain and Germany went to war. At first there was considerable national fervour on both sides, soon dispelled in the mud and blood of the trenches and the terrible loss of young life. In Germany, jingoistic citizens, including thousands of Jews whether Zionists, anti-Zionists, orthodox or liberal, were called up or volunteered for the armed services. Bernhard Guttmann had done National Service as a young man and volunteered at once, becoming a member of the Landsturm Battalion, equivalent of the Home Guard but with active combat duties. Ludwig's cousin, Felix Bohm, who was a paediatrician, became a regimental officer. He received the Iron Cross first-class right at the beginning of the war for an act of outstanding courage: braving a hail of bullets, he rescued his wounded regimental commanding officer from the battlefield.

Apart from his father's active service, young Guttmann's life was changed drastically by the war. At school many of the younger teachers joined up and were replaced by older colleagues. Each day, before lessons, the latest war news was discussed:

'Being historically minded I was interested in all the events and became a kind of "war correspondent" for my class, naturally with special reference to the movements of my father's battalion. There was a time in autumn of 1914 when the Russian Central Army Group, called "Steam Roller", Dampfwalze, had progressed so near to the Silesian-Austrian border that these Home Guard battalions took part in the defence of the Silesian frontier. Many of the new regiments had been hurriedly transferred to East Prussia where, later in 1914, the Russian Army Group under General Rennen-kamp was wiped out by the German Army Group under the command of General Hindenburg, later to become President of Germany under the Nazi regime.'

The situation in Silesia in 1914 in fact became so dangerous that boys of sixteen and above were evacuated. If the Russians had occupied Upper Silesia, even temporarily, the First World War could hardly have lasted its four years of unspeakable human destruction. Guttmann's closest friends and relatives were caught up in the slaughter:

'Of my own family, my cousin Max Schafer, married with two children, was killed at the Somme, and Hans Bobrecker at Paschendale at the age of eighteen. My closest school friend and playmate during childhood, a highly gifted boy, Walter Mohr – he and his parents lived in my father's house – was called up in 1916 and gassed in 1917 on the Somme, and soon died. He was one year older than me. He wrote me a postcard from his hospital bed, the words at the end of the card becoming more and more indistinguishable.

'In 1916 the German youth movement was transformed into a pre-military organisation and we were drilled by soldiers in preparation for the Army. At that time, the pupils in the higher classes of our school had also to take part in a population census, and I was given a district of coalminers. What I saw there of poverty, destitution, drunkenness, squalor and misery imprinted itself on my memory for ever and made me socially conscious for the rest of my life.'

At the beginning of 1917 Ludwig Guttmann had his first medical for Army call-up and was classified fit for service in the infantry. Soon afterwards a regulation was passed to the effect that all boys in High School who were A1 medically could take their school leaving examinations early, on condition that they joined the National Emergency Services pending call-up. By this time there were acute shortages of personnel throughout Germany, particularly in industry and in the hospitals. Impatient to be getting on with his life, Guttmann seized the opportunity:

'Because of my disillusions with the years spent at High School, despite some bright and lucid moments, I took immediate advantage of this regulation. As I had wanted to become a doctor since I was very young, I joined the Accident Hospital for Coalminers, Knappschafts-Lazarett, in Königshütte, as an orderly.'

Situated in the centre of the coalmining and foundry area, this hospital was large – it had eight hundred beds – and was the first of its kind in the world, many of its patients having traumatic injuries of the central nervous system, including industrial spinal injuries. During the war it was also being used as an auxiliary military hospital for casualties from the Eastern Front. Guttmann was just eighteen when he became an orderly. He remembered that 'the smoke of the ironworks sometimes developed into pea-soup fog, even worse than the notorious London smog, causing classic respiratory disturbances. Pneumokoniosis, a disease stemming from lungs scarred by inhaling coal dust, was a common disease among coalminers.' He carried bedpans, made beds and cleaned wards which 'helped me quite a lot later, as a doctor, to supervise my nurses'. He also assisted during surgery, holding the rather primitive lights for the surgeon and handing retractors. But this was not until the fourth operation he witnessed; during the first three he had to be taken out of the theatre – 'I couldn't look at blood . . .'

A curious episode touched the young Guttmann at the Accident Hospital, though it was a long time before he would appreciate its significance. A previous Medical Director of the hospital, Professor Wagner, had published in 1898 a textbook on injuries of the spine and spinal cord, based on the case histories of some five hundred and sixty-four patients. In it, he advocated 'conservative management of the broken spine and spinal cord injury in the acute stage, with only rare indications for surgery':

'When I entered the Accident Hospital as an orderly I did not imagine in my wildest dreams that some fifty years later, from my own experience as a neurosurgeon, I would come to the same conclusion as Wagner expressed in his monograph. In those days, I had not the faintest knowledge that the monograph existed . . .'

It was also in the Accident Hospital that Guttmann had his first personal – and poignant – experience of a severe spinal cord injury patient. *He never forgot it*:

'A well built, over six foot tall young coalminer was admitted with a broken back and complete paraplegia below the waist. The patient was held in a supine position in the air by four strong men. Two pulled on his legs and two on his arms with the aid of towels fixed under the patient's armpits, while the surgeon realigned the bone forcibly with his right fist from below. Thereafter the patient was put into a plaster cast and transferred to the surgical ward, and screened off from other patients.

'One of the assisting doctors told me, in passing, that this man would be dead in six weeks at the latest. I, incredulous, asked the reason for this sad prognosis. "Just watch him – you will see and learn" was his laconic reply. During the following weeks I saw this fine, strong man rapidly deteriorate and become increasingly emaciated as a result of sepsis from urinary infection and sloughing, multiple bedsores, until he died just five weeks after his injury. Although, during future years of my career, I saw many more such victims suffering the same fate, it was the picture of that young man which remained indelibly fixed in my memory.'

Guttmann was also expected to do some work at the hospital as a clerk. One of his duties was to gain a rudimentary knowledge of modern Greek. During the First World War Greece was a neutral country, but a Greek Army Corps had nevertheless gone over to the German side. Their reward was to be used as coalminers in Upper Silesia replacing German miners, many of whom were in the armed forces. It was Guttmann's job to take the case histories of Greeks who reported sick to the hospital.

One Greek soldier arrived with a septic throat and high temperature, an illness so severe he later died from it. While

Guttmann asked questions about his symptoms the man was seized by a fit of coughing and Guttmann received the full blast. Not surprisingly, he soon went down with a temperature and septic tonsillitis. After three weeks of illness he went back to work, though still feeling poorly. Far from improving, his voice became more and more hoarse and he developed a swelling on the right side of his neck. On one of his routine rounds the hospital Medical Director spotted this, diagnosed its cause and operated immediately. A large abscess was opened and a glass tube inserted for drainage. When the tube was withdrawn and the wound closed, high temperatures and another abscess returned. Guttmann had five similar operations but while the tube was in place he was fairly fit and able to work.

By the end of 1917 the economic situation in Germany was deteriorating rapidly. Despite strict rationing there were increasing shortages of basic foods, resulting in hostile demonstrations by coalminers and other workers, and their wives. During the last two years of the war the black market had developed steadily. Many foods and drinks were made from 'ersatz', imitation, products. Bread, made largely from potatoes, was crumbly and tasted bitter; the best available at the time was called 'Kommissbrot', the Army bread given to soldiers, many of whom sold their ration to civilians. Certain vegetables such as turnips, which in Germany had previously been regarded as only fit for animals, became a staple of everyday diet. Guttmann's mother kept chickens and acquired a goat, milking it herself to eke out the family's meagre food supplies.

In November 1917 Guttmann received his call-up papers and presented himself at the 156th Infantry Regiment in the nearby town of Beuthen. He was waiting with a group of people – boys of his own age and older people whose services were now needed – when the inspecting officer spotted the bandage around his neck. On being told of the glass drainage tube, still in place beneath it, he sent Guttmann packing off home with the words: 'We have enough cripples here!' So Guttmann's first attempt to join the German Army was unsuccessful. He was, as he said himself, 'war disabled, without having worn a uniform . . .' But his attitude towards serving his own country was unequivocal. He spoke vehemently in the Imperial War Museum on the subject many years later as an honoured citizen of another land: 'Of course I wanted to do something for my country . . . my father was in the Army . . . we were a very patriotic family.'

Freiburg and Breslau,
1918-28

LEAVING HIS WORK as an orderly, Guttmann began his medical studies at the University of Breslau on 1 April 1918. Now called Wroclaw, Breslau was then the capital of Silesia, an imposing city built along the banks of the Oder and dating from the eighth century. In the 1400s it had been sacked by the Mongols, and afterwards rebuilt in Gothic style. Many remarkable buildings were preserved until the Second World War when the Nazis turned the city into a fortress. Their resistance to the Russians, which lasted for eighty days, again wrecked the city and caused terrible loss of life among its inhabitants. However, the magnificent crenellated Ratskeller, city hall, survived; the university, founded in 1702, was also little damaged.

Guttmann discovered very quickly that his experience at the Accident Hospital stood him in good stead and 'dispelled the lyrical concept I had acquired of the medical profession'. The tutorial system as it is known in Britain did not exist in German universities at that time, so as an undergraduate he was expected to find his own way with very little guidance as to how best to organise his studies.

'One of the subjects in which I registered at Breslau was anatomy, including, in the winter term, the dissection course of cadavers under the direction of Professor Kallius, a distinguished-looking man always immaculate in his cut-away coat and often surrounded by attractive and worshipping female students. Some lecturers and professors were still in uniform, as were many of the students.'

All his life Ludwig Guttmann sought and admired excellence. He demanded it of himself and of those who worked for him, and took great pride in the achievements of professors and scientists at the universities with which he was associated. He never forgot those who had made names for themselves at Breslau: the surgeon, von Mikulicz; the opthamologist Utoff; the gynaecologist Kastner; and the neuropsychiatrist Wernicke, and his pupils Foerster and Bonhoeffer. The latter became Professor of Psychiatry in Berlin; one of his sons, a priest, was involved in the coup d'etat against Hitler in June 1944 and was hanged. Another pupil of Wernicke was Goldstein, who became Professor of Neurology in Berlin, one of the first Jewish professors to be imprisoned by the Nazis.

Guttmann was delighted to be a part of this great university. But unfortunately as he was settling to his studies he came down with an attack of a dangerous virus which was sweeping Europe, known as Spanish 'flu. The virus proved fatal for thousands – particularly young and healthy men – and triggered serious complications, some of which could result in Parkinson's disease later in life. But Ludwig Guttmann was lucky. During the severe part of his illness the glass tube still draining the abscess on his neck was removed. Thanks to good nursing by his landlady, he recovered 'and during the 'flu a miracle happened: the old wound in my neck closed and never broke down again. The virulent 'flu virus must have overpowered those bacteria which were responsible for that protracted infection.'

As a German, a Jew and a doctor, religious intolerance, in medicine particularly, came to be of profound interest to Ludwig Guttmann:

'In medicine and science, Jews who adhered to their faith were as a rule barred from attaining the summit of their academic careers, namely that of becoming Professor Ordinarius – professor of a University chair – unless they agreed to renounce their faith. Amongst those professors at Breslau University who had renounced their Jewish religion to further their careers was Minkowski, Professor of Medicine, who discovered the vital function of the pancreas gland in the sugar metabolism, and thus was often called the "grandfather" of insulin. Another was the pharmacologist Riesser, the grandson of Gabriel Riesser who came from a distinguished Rabbinical family. Gabriel Riesser had been one of the few Jewish members of the first German National Assembly in Frankfurt in 1848, and a valiant fighter for Jewish emancipation.'

But even during the democratic Weimar Republic when Guttmann was a student religious intolerance in German universities was still widespread. It had also taken an increasingly nationalistic turn, with slander and ugly acts of violence directed at the minority group of Jewish students, as Guttmann soon discovered:

'I attended student meetings then in Breslau as a member of my fraternity Thuringia, at which our members, including those with war decorations for bravery or with severe disabilities from war wounds, who tried to stand up against senseless accusations were shouted down and even physically attacked. It was clear that Democrats and Jews had become scapegoats for the defeat of the mighty German Army in the First World War. Pride damaged by this defeat was soothed by misleading propaganda which insinuated that Germany had not been beaten but had been betrayed by traitors on the home front.'

When he matriculated at the Medical Faculty of Breslau University, Guttmann had joined the Jewish Fencing Fraternity, Thuringia, founded in 1901 as a member of KC and styled on the fraternity Viadrina; this had begun in Breslau in 1886 at the height of a wave of anti-semitism throughout the German universities, when Jewish students who were members of many fraternities were asked to resign:

'Ten medical and one theological student decided to set up their own fencing fraternity, Viadrina, with all the usual traditions including duelling. They wore their own colours, caps and sashes to be openly recognisable as Jews. In those days this was an act of bravery, for these young students were only a tiny minority standing up against the religious and racial prejudices which bedevilled the vast majority of students in Germany. Their fraternity was not just the foundation of another student club but the creation of an idea which in those days was unique – namely, to fight as Jews against anti-semitism in the universities. Their banner, colours, cap and sash were certainly not an empty imitation of forms and customs of their fellow students, but a proud public demonstration of their heritage and faith.

'Their motto was the same as that inserted in stone at the entrance to Edinburgh Castle: *Nemo me impune lacessit* (Nobody will insult me unpunished). In due course, the members of the Viadrina made their mark as first-class fencers and duellists in their encounters, called Mensur, against their opponents. This medieval custom was upheld traditionally in German Universities (and still is!), and, although officially forbidden, the authorities concerned turned a blind eye (and still do!).'

When Guttmann returned to Konigshutte for his summer vacation in July 1918 he was given another medical for the Army, and again classified A1. He received his call-up papers for the 6th Artillery Regiment in Breslau on 9 November, but when he reported for duty he was turned away. The war had ended at last. This was his second and last attempt to join the German Army. 'And so,' Guttmann concluded, 'thus ended my military "career", as an act of God.'

In the post-war spring of 1919 Ludwig Guttmann left Breslau University to study at Freiburg, the lovely ancient city in the Black Forest with its beautiful cathedral. He remained there until 1923 when he took and passed his final examinations. At that time, he noted meticulously, the Medical Faculty at Freiburg had many outstanding members including Lexer, Professor of Surgery; Aschoff, probably the most famous pathologist in the world; and von Kries, Professor of Physiology, well-known through his work on the physiology of the vision. Guttmann remembered vividly that:

'Aschoff was an outstanding scientist and a brilliant teacher, and his style and eloquence made his lectures most popular and inspiring. Many post-graduates from other countries became his pupils and for some years he set aside a special room for the Japanese ... Lexer's lectures were excellent and very instructive. He was a heftily built man who at times could be pretty hard on ignorant students as well as on members of his own staff. He held the strong, though not generally accepted, view that wound infections during operations were mainly caused by the surgeon and his assistant talking during the operation, and that the chief collector of bacteria was the mask through which they talked. Therefore he and his assistants did not wear masks or caps, but the operation was carried out in strict silence on the part of everyone; instruments etc. were requested by hand and finger signals only.

'In view of the frequent outbursts of shouting behind his mask by my future teacher in Neurosurgery, Professor Foerster, during brain and spinal cord operations, and the extremely rare wound infections which ensued, I was not surprised that Lexer's rigid view in this respect was rejected by most surgeons. Lexer had strong nationalistic views and was one of the professors in Germany at that time who wanted to free the German language from foreign words. One had to be careful not to use foreign words when reporting an exam case as I, to my great discomfort, discovered. I was reporting the history of a case where a girl of nineteen had fallen from a "balcony". He stopped me angrily: "Start again." I finally and with great relief and sweat found the adequate German word, *Geländer*.'

In Freiburg, Guttmann joined the respected KC fraternity called Ghibellinia. He found the rivalry and the religious intolerance among the Freiburg students and fraternities slightly less intense than those of Breslau, but it was there that he witnessed an act of anti-semitism so distressing to him that he never forgot:

'The Rector of Freiburg University arranged a procession of all student fraternities to a monument erected in honour of those students of Freiburg University killed in the First World War. My Freiburg fraternity had lost eleven per cent of its members, including one at the famous sea battle at Skagerak in 1916; a pretty high percentage compared with other fraternities. Led by their Presidents and second and third office holders, the student fraternities marched alphabetically in full dress and colours. Behind my fraternity followed the notoriously anti-semitic corporation Marcomannia-Abertia. It was soon noticed that this fraternity deliberately kept a distance which increased more and more in spite of two warnings by our President who, by the way, had become an officer in the war and was decorated with the Iron Cross first-class for bravery.

'In view of the solemnity of the occasion our President certainly tried to avoid trouble, despite this incredibly offensive attitude, but as his repeated requests to close up were ignored he slapped the face of his counterpart. Naturally, the incident was reported to the Rector who made the judgement of reprimanding *both* parties for misdemeanour, totally ignoring the cause.'

As the 1920s progressed, the ever-present religious prejudice changed into a malign nationalism, arising out of the bitterness of the German defeat in the war and the punitive measures forced upon the country in the Treaty of Versailles in 1918. Lacking military power and economically weak, Germans looked inward for self-definition, for reaffirmation of past and perhaps largely imagined glories. There can be no doubt that the seeds of modern German anti-semitism were rooted in this attitude.

To Ludwig Guttmann, the unmistakeable signs of national paranoia were everywhere. Hooliganism was accepted. Student fencing corporations passed a resolution 'refusing satisfaction with weapons to Jews and Negroes'. 'One could sometimes find in the morning slogans such as "Jews Out" painted or stuck on buildings during the night.' Jewish students were frequently set upon by mobs of rowdies: 'Already, in 1922, one could occasionally see students in Freiburg wearing the swastika ...'

In general the academic staff, including the professors, appeared indifferent to such behaviour. Some, who had themselves been members of reactionary fencing fraternities, were openly sympathetic. Guttmann and his fellow students at Freiburg saw no evidence of firm moral leadership taken against it, but there were individual lecturers and professors who abhorred the rising racial and nationalistic tensions:

'One of these was my teacher in general medicine, Professor de la Camp, himself a former member of an old fencing fraternity. One day, when lecturing, he stopped in front of a student, pointed to a swastika on his lapel and told him sharply: "Take that thing off. You are not in a political meeting but supposed to be learning medicine."'

It was a time of growing political unease. Guttmann was an enthusiastic student, a young man of broad interests and tremendous energy: 'It would be quite wrong to imagine that these tribulations prevented us from enjoying our student years to the full.' There was plenty of activity within the fraternity – opportunities for sport, well-chaperoned dances and weekends spent hiking in the surrounding Black Forest. Regular evening meetings took place between full fraternity members, called fellows, and freshmen, who were known as foxes. Fraternity members lunched together daily in the popular Freiburg restaurant Kopf, Head, after morning lectures. Punctuality was mandatory – latecomers had to pay a small fine to the treasurer unless they could provide good reason – and a smart appearance was appreciated.

Lectures were given by the Fuchsmajor, Fox Major, an older student whose standing in the fraternity was highest after the President. These lectures centred on Jewish history in general and on the backgrounds of the various fraternities. At that time the Jewish fraternities, although entirely loyal to the Jewish faith, were not Zionist supporters. Guttmann was elected Fox Major twice.

Fencing was an important activity at the university and became Guttmann's favourite sport, one at which he excelled: he bore facial scars for the rest of his life as proof:

'I did not approve of duels, whether "friendly" or in earnest, although on entering the KC I had accepted this practice and had my share of duelling bouts, as well as acting as secundant in them for other fencers. This I found more interesting, as one had to watch not only the correct fencing of one's own fellow but also that of his opponent and his secundant, and had to be quick to intercept with sabre

39

or rapier to protect one's fencer against incorrect hits or behaviour by the opponent or his secundant.

'In a "friendly" fencing contest in Breslau with the long rapier, *Schlager*, against a member of an inter-denominational fencing fraternity called Alemania, I tried a special hit which left my face unprotected. My secundant failed to fall in to intercept and catch my opponent's stroke and as a result I received a large cut to the left side of my face and later another on my left forehead, and retired from the contest at the order of the supervising doctor. I had thirteen stitches put in by the doctor, the "anaesthetic" being carried out, as was the custom, by a fellow student pressing his thumbs hard into my ears, the greater discomfort of which somewhat counteracted the pain of the insertion of the stitches! When I returned home with these 'scars of honour', my parents, especially my mother, were not amused.'

It was during this happy period in Ludwig Guttmann's life that he met his wife-to-be, Else Samuel. Her father had had a large furniture business, first in Alsace where she was born, and later in Breslau. Else Samuel was an energetic and attractive young woman, athletic and an excellent skier. With her widowed mother and her two elder sisters she went often to the family cottage in the picturesque Black Forest. It was there in 1919 that she and Ludwig Guttmann had met and become friends. Clearly a rather progressive young woman – she was then in her last year of High School – she joined the informal rambling association which Guttmann had organised for his fellow medical students and their friends.

During these years, Else Samuel kept a series of diaries now in the possession of her daughter, Eva Loeffler. Immaculately penned between hard covers, they look so fresh they might have been written yesterday: 'I really am thrilled to bits, I find him enchanting.' Soon a pet name for him, *Lumpel*, appears when she refers to him and to the progress of their friendship. It was Lumpel who gave her 'My most beautiful birthday rose' the following July.

But among the tumble of youthful thoughts and emotions are indications of the strong-minded woman she was to become, the wife who would one day help her husband make hard decisions. Even then, despite her friends, her studies and the idyllic scenery of the Black Forest, she was politically aware. She writes, again in 1919 and no doubt after some anti-semitic event: 'These unpleasant incidents would not happen in a national Jewish state. But the idea of starting a Jewish state in Palestine is completely impossible. I love my German fatherland much, much too much for me ever to leave it.' As a wife and mother in 1939, it was she who would bargain with the Nazi authorities so that the family could leave the country – 'my German fatherland' – with at least some of their possessions. But for the present, her life was full and exciting.

Before Guttmann left for Freiburg he had become aware of the difficulties Jewish boys and girls had in joining the German Youth Movement, which developed into the notorious 'Hitler Jugend'. With a fellow medical student, Josef Hirschberg, he had founded Kameraden, Comrades, a non-political Jewish Youth Organisation for youngsters between the ages of six and seventeen:

'I started the first group in my home town Königshütte in the winter of 1918 and continued this activity in 1919 in Freiburg. This Youth Organisation, built up on the principles of the Scout Movement, developed rapidly in many cities. The Black Forest moutains were naturally ideal for our weekend and holiday excursions, with our rucksacks and guitars, meals cooked on open fires and at night sleeping in barns on straw. Singing and musical sessions with various instruments were held, resulting in two performances of

Haydn's *Children's Symphony* by thirty children, whom I trained and conducted.

'Else Samuel, with her enthusiasm and organising talents, became my successor as leader of the Freiburg Kameraden, while I spent a good deal of my time organising youth clubs in other cities in the south of Germany, becoming a "Gauleiter" of that district. The words "Fuhrer", "Gauleiter" etc. were not the invention of the Nazis but originated in the German Youth Movement, the "Wandervogel", Wanderbirds.'

With these varied social and sporting activities taking up so much of his time, Guttmann's studies, not surprisingly, suffered. His pre-clinical exams were 'nearly a disaster, which shocked me into being aware of my neglect – and that medicine was not child's play'. He realised that if he hoped to qualify as a doctor he had to concentrate on his work. Thereafter he took his studies a good deal more seriously and passed his finals in 1923 with 'almost a first'.

This academic near-miss entitled him, as the rules then were, to apply for re-examination in one of the subjects in which he had not taken a first. He decided to sit again and chose pathology. However, Professor Aschoff's response to his request was discouraging, saying quite frankly that he had already made a 'cross section' of Guttmann's knowledge and abilities, and if examined again he could only do worse. He then enquired whether Guttmann had a girlfriend. Aschoff's advice: on a lovely June day like this, forget about examinations and take her up into the Black Forest ... Sensibly, Guttmann took his counsel and contented himself with 'almost a first'.

After his finals, Guttmann completed his thesis on tracheal tumours, passed his viva and in 1924, when he returned to

Breslau, received his MD. He spent his first pre-registration months in Breslau Hospital in the department of general medicine.

This was a difficult and unsettling time for the Guttmann family. Bernhard and Dorothea had been forced in 1921 to move from Königshütte because of political unrest between Germans and Poles. The district was then occupied by troops of the Allied Commission supervising the referendum by which Upper Silesia was to be divided into German and Polish territories. It was also the height of devastating German inflation. Like many others, and despite his years of hard work, Bernhard Guttmann was forced to sell up his home and business at the worst possible time. His son remembered those months of dangerous social collapse:

'The economic and financial situation was at its lowest depth, the inflationary value of the mark fell almost daily – its value in the morning often had sunk by the evening. Therefore there was a rush, in particular by housewives, to buy as much as possible in the mornings. New money notes were printed in rapid succession from a ten thousand to a billion marks value, equivalent later to the so-called one "Rentenmark". The value of shares bought before and during the early stages of inflation sunk lower and lower. Many small businesses went into liquidation and the people who were the hardest hit were the middle and lower classes, whose living standards sank to the depths. Many families of retired professionals and pensioners had to sell their jewellery and other valuables to make ends meet, and unemployment and the number of strikes increased. Of course, profiteers exploited the sad situation.'

In Breslau the family, as so many others at that time, lived in straitened circumstances. Bernhard was able to provide his newly qualified son with only a small amount of pocket money, quickly spent on medical textbooks and other necessities. Daily he walked the two miles to and from his parents' home and the hospital.

Guttmann had decided by this time that he wanted to specialise as a paediatrician – his work with the Kameraden had stimulated his interest in the psychology of children. But the Professor of Paediatrics at the university quickly disillusioned him, saying that he already had at least one doctor per baby . . . this was the depression . . . He suggested that Guttmann continue his training at the modern municipal hospital called Wenzel Hancke Krankenhaus. He went there immediately and was sitting in the waiting-room, hoping for an interview, when an old friend from university appeared, also a young doctor, who told him flatly that there would be no job for him there in the department of general medicine. But there was a vacancy, he said, on the ground floor in Professor Foerster's department of Neurology and Neurosurgery. 'If I were you,' he said, 'I would try the floor below.'

'Somewhat dejectedly, I did so. And perhaps, more than any other, those words shaped my whole life and future career.'

Perhaps, also, memories stirred of the young coalminer he had watched die in the Accident Hospital at Königshütte some six years before, and his own sense of outrage that nothing could be done to help him. In any event, he got the job and began to train as a neurologist and neurosurgeon under Professor Otfrid Foerster on 1 October 1923. Although he did not know it, he had embarked on his life's work.

Ludwig Guttmann spent most of the following ten years working under Otfrid Foerster, a brilliant and innovative neurologist. Neither neurology nor neurosurgery were then recognised as individual specialities; neurology was included in departments of psychology or general medicine and neuro-surgery was carried out by general surgeons. Foerster's neurological unit at Wenzel Hancke Krankenhaus in Breslau was exceptional, considered the most advanced in Europe. As a scientist, Foerster had complete mastery of the anatomy and physiology of the nervous system. His surgery, although frequently successful, was less highly regarded by fellow neurosurgeons, at least one of whom considered his methods 'ungainly'.

However, Foerster's reputation in Europe was so high that he was called to treat Lenin in Moscow when he developed paralysis with speech disturbances. He stayed in Moscow, with some intervals, from 1922 to 1928, and was in fact there when Guttmann first arrived at the unit to start work as his voluntary unpaid assistant; the following year he became his full-paid assistant or registrar. The chief assistant, whom Foerster trusted implicitly, was Dr Otto Schwab, with whom Guttmann immediately began a close friendship.

When Foerster was asked one day why he had so many Jewish assistants, he replied that he was 'more interested in intelligence than religion', but Guttmann's first encounter with 'that great man' was far from promising. Foerster had just returned from visiting his illustrious patient in Moscow. Exhausted, he came straight to an arduous operation:

'I saw a haggard and tense-looking, skinny man, entering the scrubbing-up room of the operation theatre without taking any notice of his medical staff, with the exception of the two doctors designated to assist at a brain operation, the first I had ever attended. Most operations were carried out using local anaesthetic. The patient was a youngster with a cerebellar tumour in the front part of the brain. The oper-ation was difficult and Foerster highly irritable. I pitied the theatre sister who had to bear with him, which she did with remarkable stoicism. The tumour turned out to be malignant and when, after the operation, the patient was turned from the prone to the supine position, he died. I had to hold the patient's legs during the turning, and Foerster bellowed at me – the first time he had taken any notice of my existence – that I was holding the legs incorrectly. When he left the theatre obviously very upset, Schwab insisted that I should go to his room to introduce myself, which I did with some apprehension. To my amazement Foerster greeted me in quite a friendly way and immediately gave me a short lecture on the difficulty of operations in the cerebellar region.'

Foerster was an extremely hard taskmaster, addicted to intensive clinical work as well as to research, and drove himself just as hard as his assistants. An eighteen-hour day was normal for his neurological team. He would telephone after operations at any time, even at five in the morning, to enquire of the medical officer in charge the details of a patient's condition, all of which he was expected to know:

'He caught me only once unprepared and on all later occasions I informed myself fully of the patient's condition before I went to the telephone to report. He would always apologise, "Sorry to disturb you but I am worried about X ..." Foerster's routine was to operate at 9 a.m. in his private clinic assisted only by Schwab and, later, myself. About 11 a.m. or later, we went by taxi to the confectioner's closest to the hospital, where we had coffee and pastries. After this short relaxation we went back to the hospital where he either made his clinical rounds or operated on another case for two to three hours. He then went home for a meal, which he often took alone, and afterwards saw his private patients there. He was a heavy cigarette smoker and on one occasion advised a private patient with a vascular disease to give up smoking. When the surprised patient exclaimed, "Sir, since I consulted you today you have already smoked six cigarettes!" Foerster, slightly annoyed, retorted: "Do I consult you or you me?"'

The lighting techniques during operations were still quite primitive and became 'a nightmare' for the assistant with the daunting task of illuminating the incision with a headlamp: 'He had to develop the skill of shining the light into the depths of the wound, without burning the surgeon's neck or obstructing his line of vision. To do that for two hours or longer was most exhausting.' Foerster's department became a Mecca for neurologists and neurosurgeons from other parts of Germany and, indeed, from all over the world.

Guttmann was naturally much influenced by Foerster's methods and outlook. Foerster's method was first to understand how the body works before studying what had gone wrong – and then apply his findings to his patients. During his neurological training, Guttmann developed an interest in the physiology of sweat glands, which became his special subject of research and later the thesis to support his application for a chair at the Medical Faculty at Breslau University; he continued this research in Oxford. Another subject which interested him deeply was electro-diagnosis and therapy, which became particularly important in the treatment of some kinds of nerve, spinal or polio patients, to substitute and improve by direct electrical stimulation the lost function of the paralysed muscles. This experience, too, helped him many years later in Oxford when he was conducting experimental research on peripheral nerve injuries in animals.

Guttmann's successful assistantship with Foerster ended in March 1928. Anxious about his future, he had applied for a Rockefeller scholarship but was told that they had already been allocated for the year. This turned out to be a lucky disappointment, for at exactly that time Guttmann heard through a friend that Professor Weygandt, Director of the

47

University Department of Psychiatry and Neurology in Hamburg, had set up a special operating theatre unit in the huge State mental hospital there, Friedrichsberg, and was looking for a young neurosurgeon to run it. Guttmann applied. Four days later he was offered the job. He accepted.

This was a tremendously exciting period in his life. At twenty-eight, he had been offered the most challenging professional position he could have anticipated. His very appointment was historic: he was, in fact, the first neurosurgeon in the world working and operating in a psychiatric hospital.

In 1927 he had married Else Samuel, the girlfriend of his Freiburg university days, and in the spring of 1928 the couple settled in Hamburg, with high hopes for the future.

Hamburg and Breslau, 1928-33

From the first, Guttmann's work at Freidrichsberg absorbed him. The three thousand patients gave him immense scope – 'fantastic material', as he put it. In addition to his neuro-surgical work he was also gaining firsthand experience in psychiatry and neuro-pathology. As he had done previously with Foerster, he was carrying out explorations of the brain and wrote vividly and enthusiastically of an aspect of his work with which he experienced considerable success at that time, and which interested him profoundly:

'My surgical procedures, in addition to operations of brain tumours both benign and malign, revealed most interesting observations, especially amongst patients suffering from cerebral palsy combined with epilepsy. Remarkably good results were achieved by excisions of scars or cysts of the grey matter of the brain.

'In view of the low threshold of central irritability of epileptics, anti-convulsant drugs were used to deal with the general irritability and it was most interesting to find that the smallest doses kept the patient free from seizures whereas before the operation even the largest doses had proved ineffective while having very adverse effects on the mental condition.

'Another remarkably beneficial effect of the surgical treatment of epilepsy was the mental improvement of the patient.

As an example the following case may be quoted: a nineteen-year-old boy, born with a weakness on the right side of his body, had suffered from epilepsy since the age of seven as the result of an accident. In due course the seizures increased in number and intensity in spite of drugs in increasing dosage. During the last year he had sometimes had twenty-nine fits per day, associated with severe irritability and aggression. On repeated occasions he had tried to jump from a window and abscond from hospital. The epileptic attacks were always uniform, originating from the left side of the brain. In fact there was enlargement of the left lateral brain cavity, indicating a scarring condition of the left hemisphere of the brain.

'At operation, the exposed brain at first showed no pulsation and revealed a large cystic formation of the whole central region, separated from the adjacent macroscopically normal cerebral area by a firm scar. Having elicited an epileptic attack electrically from this part of the brain, I opened the large cyst, which did not communicate with the left ventricle, and excised the large porus and the adjacent area.

'For a short time after the operation the boy still had a few attacks which, however, ceased completely as soon as drug therapy with very small doses of barbiturates was commenced. The paralysis of the right side remained, of course, unchanged, but there was not the slightest motor speech disturbance that one would expect temporarily after such an excision. However, the most striking improvement was in the patient's mental condition. Whilst before the operation he was either lying dull and apathetic in bed, or behaving either childishly, excitably and unmanageably, he became a reasonable, co-operative young man, acting at first as a reliable errand-boy and later taking up office training.'

As this acutely observed case history of one of his patients at the time indicates, Guttmann quickly rose to the challenge of his highly responsible position. However, he had barely had time to adjust to his new life and work in Hamburg when, in August 1929, terrible news reached him. His close friend in Breslau, Otto Schwab, had died suddenly. It was a horrifying story: 'Rozy, Otto's beautiful wife, also a doctor, had died in childbirth fever. In utter despair he had committed suicide, taking his baby with him.'

A few weeks later, still stunned by the tragedy, Guttmann received an imploring letter from Otfrid Foerster, asking him to return to Breslau to take Schwab's place. Ironically, this crisis of decision came just as Guttmann had arranged a six months' sabbatical in the United States to study the technique of the famous neurosurgeon, Cushing, in Boston. It was 'a dilemma ... a crossroads of my life'. On the one hand he had, at Friedrichsberg, an unparalleled opportunity, complete charge of his own department and was utterly fascinated by the range of work. At a young age he was already building a reputation for himself in a rapidly developing branch of medicine. Surely such an opportunity would not recur? On the other hand, Otfrid Foerster was his teacher, the man to whom he felt he owed everything. And loyalty was – and remained – Guttmann's byword.

There was another important consideration also – Else, now settled into her first married home and expecting their first child. What were her feelings in this crucial decision he was called upon to make so unexpectedly? 'It was my wife, really, who was determined and helped me in this difficulty.' Together, the Guttmanns decided to return to Breslau, something he never regretted. It was, he believed, 'a question of loyalty only', but the poignancy of Schwab's death, coming at a time when he and Else were starting a family of their own, may also have influenced them. At any rate, Guttmann gave his notice at Friedrichsberg, cancelled his planned sabbatical in Boston and made arrangements to return to Breslau.

Guttmann's return to the Wenzel Hancke Krankenhaus was quite different from his first appearance there in 1923 as an unpaid assistant. He was now Foerster's associate and with the additional experience gained at the psychiatric hospital in Hamburg, felt himself competent to work on an equal footing, running a department which had increased to a hundred beds. Foerster had no hesitation in delegating major operations to him, as he had promised when asking him to return. Guttmann's thesis on the neuro-regulation of sweat glands was accepted by the Medical Faculty at Breslau University and in 1930 he received the *Venia Legende* as Professor in Neurology. Despite the preceding upheavals in both their lives, he and Foerster quickly formed a partnership of mutual respect and medical innovation:

'My new position demanded, in addition to lecturing and assisting Foerster at operations in his private clinic, much hard work in many aspects of the running and administration of the clinical department. Many neurologists and neuro-surgeons from all over the world visited the unit to study our methods. It was to a great extent left to me to take them round the wards, where patients and their problems were discussed, indeed a very time-consuming activity. Naturally, I had plenty of opportunity to increase my surgical experience not just in brain surgery but, in particular, spinal cord and spinal root surgery, as well as operations on the nerves which control blood vessels, the gut, and other organs whose functions we are not aware of but which are essential to life.'

Guttmann describes such an operation in which both he and Foerster were involved at this time. He had operated not knowing what he might find and came upon a condition of extreme rarity. His notes give an accurate account of the state of neurosurgery in Germany around 1930, the limitations as well as the high degree of skill:

'While Foerster was away, a forty-one-year-old woman was admitted, having been suffering for a year from pain between the shoulder blades and developing gradually an almost complete paraplegia below the breasts. Tests showed partial destruction of the second thoracic vertebra and an incomplete block at the level of the third. At operation I exposed a reddish-blue tumour of the outside membrane of the brain in front of the spinal cord. It was only possible to make a partial removal of the tumour because of an unusually profuse haemorrhage. The two removed pieces were sent to the department of pathology for diagnosis. A few days later I was rung up by Professor Heinrichsdorf, the pathologist, who jokingly though somewhat cynically said, to my amazement: "Congratulations, my good chap, this is the first case I have known where a goitre has been operated on from behind!"

'Actually the patient had neither a goitre nor any symptoms of thyroid gland dysfunction. In fact it was one of the rare cases of embryonic scattered thyroid "seedlings" at that level of the vertebral column which occasionally may develop into a tumour. When Foerster returned and heard the story he made another attempt at total removal of the tumour – alas with the same negative result. Retrospectively, it was the lack of a proper diathermy apparatus* which, although in the 1930s was routinely used in neurosurgery in the USA, had not yet reached Germany, which was the reason for our operative failure. The patient underwent intensive radiotherapy and the paraplegia greatly improved.'

---

* High frequency electric currents to produce heat in the deeper tissues of the body.

After the trauma of Schwab's death and the decision to leave Friedrichsberg, Ludwig and Else settled happily back in Breslau. In July 1929 their son, Dennis, was born 'two hours too late to be presented to me by Else as my thirtieth birthday gift'. Four years later they had a daughter, Eva.

In those days, Breslau was still a delightful city with wide, tree-lined streets and beautiful parks and was well-known for its excellent modern department stores. The Guttmanns lived in a spacious flat with servants to help with the children and housework. A devoted mother, Else's life was naturally centred on home and family. Ludwig's success as an influential young doctor gave them considerable prestige in the community, and they had a busy social life – dinner parties, concerts and soirees.

Meanwhile, Guttmann was developing a close personal as well as professional relationship with Foerster, as his recollections show:

'Although, in the clinical department, the distance between chief and associate was strictly observed, it was during the many evenings I spent with him either at his home or, more frequently, in one of his three favourite restaurants, that this close relationship was manifested. He would ring me up almost regularly every second or third evening, asking whether we could meet in one of these restaurants. We started with champagne, and I really became aware of the stimulating effect of that wine, especially if we were both exhausted from long operations or other work. This was followed by a light meal and wine. Foerster was a connoisseur of exquisite wines, his favourite being Palatina. At his home, he would take from his wine cellar bottles of highly selected wines and explain to me in detail their origin, flavour, etc.

'On these evenings, when discussing some problems of patients in the department, Foerster could not only tolerate my sometimes different views but actually found them stimulating for his own reasoning. I had the opportunity to share his thoughts and to watch the working of his extraordinary mind. These meetings would last until 11 or 12 p.m. when we would return home, relaxed, in order to be ready to start operating in Foerster's private clinic at 9 or 9.30 the next morning.

'Sometimes, if there were special visitors to the department, often from abroad, they would join us on these evenings and add to the stimulating discussions. On other occasions, he would invite a special guest to a day-long excursion in which his wife and my wife would also take part. On Christmas Eve, he and Mrs Foerster would appear in the unit with presents for his senior nursing staff, and the medical staff and patients would take part in the celebration.'

During these years, so professionally rewarding and domestically happy for the Guttmanns, the political scene in Germany was rapidly changing and most dangerously:

'The outstanding personality of the CV was Ludwig Hollander. He became a lawyer and later a legal adviser, a member of the Council and finally Director of the CV. I met him after the First World War at the annual KC Congress in Berlin and listened to his inspiring opening address. He was a brave and outspoken man, realising earlier than most that when Hitler was discharged in 1924 from Landsberg prison after his misfired coup d'état in Munich in 1923, the danger of National Socialism to the German people had not been eliminated, but only postponed.

'Hollander incessantly warned and appealed to the healthy forces of the nation to make them aware of the systematic Nazi propaganda of lies and brutality. Those resulted, alas, in making the majority of people, including the intellectuals and middle classes, gradually indifferent and insensitive. Even in 1932, when the danger of the Nazis taking over the Government became more acute, Hollander clearly foresaw the tragic consequences, and in an article in the CV newpaper of June 1932 expressed his view with courage:

"The new National Socialism means the end of all law and victory of the power of a State which is based on brutal violence ... The aim of National Socialism is to make all intellectual life uniform. It degrades man to the level of the beast.'"

On 30 January 1933 Adolph Hitler became Chancellor of Germany in a National Socialist-Nationalist coalition government. As one of many who had watched these events and this leader with increasing apprehension, Guttmann recalled:

'Hitler's public speeches became more violent, as he worked himself up into a frenzy, shaking a threatening fist or throwing his arms upwards or sideways. He had cast such a spell over the media that at the end the mass of people were in a state of psychomanic excitement.' In Germany in the 1930s, Hitler's was a corrupting power, appealing to the dark fears and hatreds of the majority, but by no means all, of the German people.

In one of his early speeches, referring to the Jews, Hitler shouted sarcastically: 'Den Juden wird kein haar gekrumt' ('Not a hair of Jews will be twisted'). He left the actual harassment to his front men, Josef Goebbels and the bestial Julius Streicher, who was eventually hanged by the Allies. Streicher published bloodthirsty and obscene tirades against the Jews in his notorious newspaper *Der Sturmer*, The Assailant, resulting in almost daily attacks by the 'Brownshirts' against defenceless people, and initiating a nationally organised boycott against Jewish shops on 1 April 1933.

The bullies and the braggarts of Guttmann's university days were being listened to now. It was to them that the power of the state had been transmitted through Hitler and the Nazi party. From the first, the National Socialists were implacably committed to realising the myth of the Herrenrasse, Master Race, or, as it was officially described, the 'co-ordination' of all aspects of German life. Those who found themselves unacceptable to the Nazi regime, not only Jews but also liberals, pacifists and dissenting conservatives, swiftly became the victims of a ruthlessly organised campaign of persecution.

Many Jews, outstanding medical men among them, during this so-called period of enlightenment remained loyal to their faith, but on attaining the rank of associate professor in their field were denied further advances in their careers.

'One such professor was Herman Oppenheim – one of the most outstanding German neurologists of his time. He was the favourite Assistant to Professor Westphal at the University Hospital Charite in Berlin, and during Westphal's long illness ran his department. Although he was nominated by the medical faculty of Berlin University to succeed Westphal as Professor Ordinarius, this nomination was rejected by the Prussian Minister of Education. Oppenheim left the Charite and opened his own private clinic, which developed into an international centre of clinical neurology. One of the congenital disorders he described, called Amyotonia Congenita, is named Oppenheim's disease.

'Another outstanding neurologist was Hugo Carl Liepman who became an honorary lecturer at Berlin University. Apparently Liepmann was told by faculty members that if he would change his name and become Protestant, a place for him as Professor Ordinents was assured. He declined.'

The statutory foundation for subsequent discrimination, both official and unofficial, was the law for the Reconstruction of the Civil Service, which was enacted in April 1933. This sweeping legislation provided that civil servants of 'non-Aryan' descent should be retired forthwith. At that time – it was refined more closely later on, in the Nuremberg racial laws – a 'non-Aryan' was anyone whose parents or grandparents were Jewish and who adhered to the Jewish faith. Myriad ordinances emanating from this law resulted in the dismissal of thousands of university and school teachers, employees in national and municipal enterprises, scientists, welfare officers and lawyers. Jewish doctors who were employed in municipal and state services were also dismissed.

Ludwig Guttmann, then in his fourth year as Foerster's associate in Breslau, was a German who happened also to be a Jew. He was a neurologist, a pioneer in the new speciality of neurosurgery, rapidly gaining an international reputation. Overnight, his work, and the basis for his family's life, were shattered:

'On 30 March 1933, while returning from a cinema in the evening, I happened to run into a doctor friend in the street. In a rather bewildered manner he told me of the news just announced, that all Jewish and Gentile non-Aryan doctors and scientists employed in hospitals, university departments or municipal institutions would be served by 31 March with notices of dismissal from their jobs. My first reaction was that of incredulity. However, 31 March revealed the cruel reality and I received my own notice, somewhat delayed, on 1 April, informing me curtly that my hospital appointment would cease on 30 June. When Foerster, who the day before had been quite convinced that this government decree would not apply to me, saw the document, he was stupefied. Recovering his self-control, he said he was determined to

see the authorities concerned as soon as possible with a view
to getting them to withdraw the notice of the dismissal.'

Guttmann was utterly shocked. Even then, he could not
comprehend the brutality of this new government which
had taken over his country. Ten days later Foerster summoned him to his office and told him he had heard from the
health authorities. They had agreed to treat Guttmann as
a special case and would suspend his notice of dismissal
temporarily until a suitable replacement could be found. For
the sake of their work together, Foerster begged him to
accept this humiliation. This man was his teacher, his friend;
he had given him total loyalty. Now he was asking for his
soul. It was a moment of despair. Discussing it forty years
later, in an interview taped for posterity, Guttmann's voice
still shook with emotion as he cried out, '*I absolutely refused.*

'What happened next was a dramatic scene which has
imprinted itself permanently on my memory. During the
previous days, I had been able to suppress my deep and
bitter feelings of helplessness in the face of all that had
happened since 1 April, the systematic defamation and suppression of the Jews in Germany through the open brut-
alities of the SA and SS hordes and the Nazi press. Now,
Foerster's extraordinary imposition was the final straw. I
completely lost my self-control and, bluntly refusing, I cried
out in an outburst of anguish and temper at Foerster: "How
could you possibly dare to make such a degrading suggestion
to me after the many years of loyalty I have given you!'
Foerster, startled and shaken by this unexpected emotional
reaction, sat down and murmured in a broken voice "What
will now happen to me and my work if you, my trusted
pupil, leave me?"'

Guttmann then calmly told Foerster that he would stay
until 30 June, the last day on which he could officially leave.
By staying on those last weeks, he forfeited the annual leave

which was due to him: many Jewish professionals in similar positions took their vacation time and left their jobs immediately. When Foerster asked him to nominate a successor, Guttmann, totally dispirited, told him the only man he could trust was Albrecht Tietze, then a neurologist in Berlin; all the other men who came to mind were confirmed Nazis. (Tietze was accepted but stayed for only eighteen months.)

During his last weeks at Wenzel Hancke Krankenhaus, Guttmann continued his work without interference. He had already made his mark and was clearly respected:

'Most members of the staff, let alone the patients, appreciated that I did not throw in the sponge and run away, and generally tried to make life easier for me. There is one incident worthy of record which shows how foreigners failed in those days to realise the seriousness of the situation.

'We had, at the time of the Nazi upheaval, visitors as usual from abroad, amongst them two English neurosurgeons, one of whom, Northfield, was a former assistant of Professor Cairns in London before the latter took up his Nuffield Professorship in Oxford. These foreign colleagues, of course, witnessed the actions of the Nazis with astonishment and bewilderment, although with complete lack of understanding. It was Northfield who, noting my grim visage in the early days of April 1933 and obviously misunderstanding the dangerous situation, asked jokingly: "Why don't you box?" I certainly was not in the mood to be teased and I flung back tersely: "Can you box against hundreds?" A fair-minded Englishman, he was immediately embarrassed by his tactlessness and saw the hopeless situation of Jews who did not have the slightest chance of an open fight, a small minority against the power of the SS and SA; and he apologised. When we met six years later at a neurological meeting in Oxford, he expressed his joy to learn that I had been spared a concentration camp.'

Guttmann walked out of the Wenzel Hancke Krankenhaus for the last time as a practising doctor of the hospital
on 30 June at six o'clock in the evening. At home later, he
was telephoned by Foerster asking him whether he would
assist at an operation in his private clinic on 2 July. He had
no legal right to do this but Guttmann understood that it
was a show of anti-Nazi defiance on Foerster's part. He
agreed. When they met at the clinic both men were naturally
depressed. Foerster said, '30 June was one of the darkest
days of my life.' Guttmann believed him. Their partnership
had been both professional and personal. They stayed in
close contact until 1939, but there was a sad epitaph to their
partnership:

'On 9 November 1933 Foerster had his sixtieth birthday.
I had organised in 1932 a commemorative jubilee volume,
or Festschrift, in his honour in the *Zeitschrift fur die gesamte
Neurologie und Psychiatrie*, of which he was the editor for
many years. Many neurologists and scientists from abroad
were invited and agreed to write papers for this occasion
but, in view of the political upheaval created by Hitler's
Government, only a few sent them. I received the Festschrift
from Springer the publisher, to present it to Foerster.

'However, the day before his birthday, Dr Altenburger,
the physiologist of the department, came to me and, rather
embarrassed, asked me "on the demand of the leading Nazi
amongst the medical staff", to hand over the Festschrift,
which was now to be presented to Foerster on the occasion
of the opening of the new research department built by the
Rockefeller Foundation.

'Naturally I refused and told Altenburger that I intended
to present the Festschrift to Foerster between nine and ten
the next morning in his home, and could be prevented from
doing so only by force. Foerster was very moved when I
presented him with the book and said: "I feel so very sad

that you, my real pupil, with whom I made all the plans for this research institute given by the Rockefeller Foundation, will not be present at the ceremony."'

Still shocked and disorientated by the loss of the job which was also his vocation, Ludwig Guttmann witnessed yet another act of Nazi ruthlessness in that year of 1933: the burning of books by Jewish and non-Aryan writers and the works of Jewish-born writers who had been subsequently baptised. The cultural legacy left to Germany by countless Jewish writers and scientists was to be eliminated, in the interests of the almighty Herrenrasse.

In Breslau, the desecration was organised by the new Rector of the university, and took place in front of the castle of Frederick the Great. Every member of the university, professors and lecturers as well as student fraternities, was required to be there. The dreadful ceremony was enacted in the evening, the area surrounding the castle illuminated by torches carried aloft by the chanting participants. Despite Else's pleadings, Ludwig decided to attend and stood, horrified, among the huge crowd of onlookers:

'After the Rector had started the procedure with a violent oration against the Jews, the huge pyre was lit with torches and the students, chorusing in disdainful perversion Max von Schenkendorff's famous freedom poem of 1819, "Freiheit, die ich meine" (Freedom, that I mean), threw hundreds of books by national authors and scientists, poets, writers, etc., on to the fire. I left the scene, sick at heart that such an act of barbarism could have ever happened in my university, where so many Jews – whether baptised or not – of almost every faculty, had made outstanding contributions to medicine, sciences, law and culture.'

It was only as he began to make his way home that he realised tears were pouring down his face, horrified by the travesty of the words 'Freiheit, die ich meine' as interpreted by the singing hordes of Nazis. Shortly thereafter, in what Guttmann considered 'the vilest step so far taken by the Nazi authorities', the *Venia Legende* of Jewish professors and lecturers, their licence to teach, were withdrawn, including his own.

The shocking suddenness with which the Nazis had moved against Jewish citizens, and the solidarity of their support among the population in general, were almost impossible to comprehend. Personal decisions had to be taken, and taken quickly: 'It was comforting, in those dreadful days, to realise that I was not forgotten.' The boycott against Jewish shops on 1 April 1933 had received worldwide publicity and condemnation. Concerned at the news coming out of Germany, many of Guttmann's foreign colleagues wrote to enquire about his plans. He received firm job offers from the United States and from Portugal. They were tempting, but he felt bitterly torn and found it hard to believe that his country 'had ceased to be a land of culture and sunk back into the worst medieval times'. By nature a fighter, the idea of leaving this country for which he felt the utmost loyalty was abhorrent to him:

'I was convinced that the Nazi regime could not last longer than two or three years, a view shared in those months by the great majority of German Jews, and indeed thousands of Christians. I therefore determined to resist as much as possible that system of suppression and cruelty ...'

His attitude, however right-minded, proved a dangerous miscalculation. In 1933 alone, approximately fifty-one thousand Jewish refugees left Germany, even though emigration was by no means easy. Travel documents were not always obtainable. Jewish properties, businesses and all assets were punitively taxed. Alarmed at the prospect of a large foreign influx, most countries passed restrictive quotas. A Jewish woman living in Breslau at the time, the wife of a lawyer, was a close family friend of the Guttmann's and with them faced the same agonising dilemma. She remembers that during the early years of the Nazi regime it was the women, the wives and mothers, who seemed more anxious to leave than their husbands, perhaps because of their protective instincts towards their children. The men, she remembers, particularly professional people of standing in the community, tended to feel that they were still needed, that they had jobs to do and must get on with them, that the political madness would pass.

This was certainly true of Ludwig Guttmann. 'I received offers from both Breslau and Hamburg Jewish Hospitals to start a department of neurology and neurosurgery. Eventually I plumped for Breslau, and started work there as head of the department on 10 July 1933.'

The Jewish Hospital in Breslau had first been built in 1760, near the city walls. As the population of Breslau increased, it was replaced by a larger hospital in 1789 and another in 1845, both in different parts of the city. In the early years of the twentieth century it became apparent that a larger and more modern building was needed. Several outstanding Jewish philanthropists raised funds for a new hospital in the southern part of Breslau, which was opened in 1903; it had a hundred and twenty beds, later increased to about four hundred:

'My neurological unit was housed in the most recently built gynaecological block, and developed within two years to a department of seventy-five beds. Later, when Jewish psychiatric patients at the order of the Nazi authorities had to be evacuated from general mental hospitals, the unit increased to about a hundred beds. Throughout the years following the setting up of the neurological department in 1933, I had a large medical staff, although only four had paid jobs, the others being younger doctors who were not allowed to continue their postgraduate studies in other hospitals. My first assistant, Hans Hauptmann – an excellent doctor, hard working, most lovable and loyal, with a promising career – was a great help in my research.

'Although Hauptmann was born and educated in Breslau, where he qualified as a doctor in the late 1920s before the Nazis came to power, he was, through his parents, of Polish nationality and in continual danger of being expelled to Poland. For several years, he was spared deportation by my intervention with the medical authorities in Breslau, but in the beginning of 1938, when the Hitler regime expelled all Jews of Polish nationality from Germany, he was forced to leave with his young wife and little son. I received only one letter from him, and I assume that he and his family perished later during the years of terror and extermination.'

Under Guttmann's direction, the neurological unit developed rapidly both medically and surgically. In addition to the variety of clinical material, there were also good facilities for his continued research. It was at the Jewish Hospital in Breslau that he introduced a new method for the investigation of the neuro-regulation of the sweat glands, the Quinizarin test, which he later used for his peripheral nerve injury research in Oxford.

A Jewish Medical Association was founded in 1934, of which Guttmann became chairman. Accounts of some of his most interesting cases were published in leading medical journals, accepted by the editors despite Nazi pressures. Guttmann himself described one of the most fascinating brain operations he performed at that time 'and one I can never forget'. His patient was a man who had been blinded in the First World War by a hand-grenade:

'At the base hospital remains of the right eye were removed, but the left eye seemed to be so completely destroyed that nothing further was done. The man made a good re-adjustment to his blindness, developing a good sense of orientation as most blind do. About several months after injury he developed irritative phenomena on the left blind eye only, consisting of lightnings and stars. He also suffered from olfactory irritation on the right side only, consisting of an abnormal smell sensation of "burning rubber". These irritation symptoms increased gradually in intensity, and under their influence his whole life-style changed dramatically. He lost his good sense of orientation and became more and more morose. This affected his family life as he became paranoid and accused his wife of letting rubber burn on the stove. He also developed attacks of unconsciousness, diagnosed as post-traumatic epilepsy, which eventually led to his admission to my unit.

'On operation a large cyst on the frontal lobe was found and opened. Both optic nerves, including chiasma, and both olfactory nerves, were exposed, the right of the latter being embedded in dense scar tissue, which was excised. The right optic nerve was very thin and atrophic, while the left optic nerve appeared practically normal, which indicated a more or less intact retina from which the optic nerve originates.

'By electrical stimulation of this optic nerve – the operation was carried out under local anaesthesia – the same, though more intensive, light phenomena from which he had been suffering was elicited. Consequently, I excised the right and left optic nerves. There was total atrophy of the right optic nerve, with complete loss of nerve fibres, while the left optic nerve was only partially abnormal or diseased. The patient was completely relieved of his irritations as well as of his 'epileptic' attacks and his family life became happy again. In due course, he regained his sense of co-ordination and as a sign of his gratitude sent me a parcel of strawberries every summer until 1938.'

Outlaws and Outcasts

THE NAZI GRIP on the country tightened. Hitler's heinous Nüremberg racial laws – 'for the protection of German blood and honour' – came into force on 1 January 1936. Jews, as well as Gentiles of mixed Jewish blood, were deprived of their civil rights, including the right to occupy any public position. As Guttmann wrote: 'We had become outlaws and outcasts of the community.' The domestic tragedies and heartbreak which followed can scarcely be imagined. 'Two daughters of my teacher, Professor Foerster, were forced to leave their student sports club because their mother was half Jewish, thus giving them one Jewish grandparent, which Hitler's insane laws designated a hallmark of Jewishness.' Many so-called 'Aryan' wives remained loyal to their Jewish husbands, and vice versa, and managed to save them from concentration camps even during the Second World War. 'Amongst these,' Guttmann remembered, 'were two of my friends. One was the wife of the head of the Orthopaedic Department at Breslau University, the other the wife of a lawyer in Königshütte. On the other hand, in some mixed marriages, Aryan husbands and wives divorced their spouses in order to keep their jobs.'

Neither was conversion to Christianity, for whatever reason, of any avail, not even to the children and grandchildren of those who had changed faith: they were designated Jews just the same and thrown out of their jobs as well as their professional, social and sport organisations.

As a further result of the racial laws, the licence to practise medicine freely as doctors or surgeons was withdrawn from Jews in August 1938, effectively expelling them from the general medical profession. They were to be known as Krankenbehandler (one who treats the sick) and permitted to treat Jews only:

'This most degrading and despicable edict showed, amongst other deprivations, how systematically the Nazis set out to destroy all civil, as well as human, rights of the Jews in Germany. Jewish passports had a large J in red colour printed on them. Men had to adopt, in addition to their forenames, the name Israel and women, Sarah, which naturally was considered by Jews as an honour and not, as intended, as an insult. Later, Jews were forced to wear an arm band with the star of David.'

That year, 1936, was a fateful year for Germany and indeed for the whole world. German troops occupied the Rhineland. 'This coup alarmed the whole of Germany, and thousands of people thought – and hoped – that the Allies would not tolerate this action but would counteract this breach of the Peace Treaty with determination to call Hitler's bluff, the more so as Germany at that time was still unprepared to risk a war. I remember very vividly the amazed disbelief, resulting in profound despair and depression, amongst thousands of people in Germany – Jews and Christians alike – at the unbelievable impotence of the Allies.'

1936 was also a sad year for Guttmann personally; his mother, whom he deeply loved and revered, died. The following year, at the age of thirty-eight, Guttmann was appointed Medical Director of the entire Jewish Hospital. It was no longer possible to ignore the Gestapo or the concentration camps into which thousands of ordinary citizens disappeared. For Jews, and for other citizens considered undesirable by the regime, life in Germany had degenerated into a nightmare. Guttmann, like many others of various religions or political faiths and backgrounds, had come to realise the extreme danger of the situation. He also realised that through his position in the hospital he had the means of helping persecuted people. This he determined to do: 'Jews or Christians – it made no difference.' He began to live a double life:

'Amongst my patients were some who were in danger of being taken by the Gestapo but whom I was able to help to escape to Czechoslovakia – indeed a rather dangerous undertaking – but the only possibility to save them from the tortures of interrogations by the Gestapo and from concentration camps. This activity created in me a strange mental state. Although fully aware of the consequences if I were caught, I continued in this activity similar to the soldier in battle. It was only when it ceased that the dangers of this mission had an emotional impact on me.

'One day, returning from a consultation in Prague to the Customs House of the German frontier, I was asked by a man in civilian clothes for a lift to Breslau. During the journey he told me he was a Customs officer who had to report to the authorities in Breslau for some investigation. A few days later I was visited in my office at home by a man in SA uniform, who enquired whether I had given a lift to a man some days previously, which I confirmed in detail. Understandably I felt very uncomfortable during the next few days and weeks, waiting for an "invitation" from the Gestapo for interrogation, but fortunately nothing further happened. In those days, there was a rather pathetic saying: "If the bell rings at 6 a.m. it is either the 'milkman' or the 'Gestapo'."'

By the end of September 1938 an extension of the government's August edict pronounced that all Gentile patients had to be discharged from Jewish hospitals or transferred to other hospitals: no Jewish doctor was permitted to treat any Gentile. Guttmann had one exception among his current patients: Dr Urutia, the Guatamalan Ambassador to Spain. Dr Urutia was recovering from a paraplegia caused by a benign tumour of the spinal cord, which Guttmann had successfully removed. Told of the new chicanery of the Nazi Government 'he was incredulous and telephoned his colleague, the Ambassador of Guatemala to Germany, who immediately protested against this inhuman edict. As a result, a telephone message from the German Foreign Office was received, cancelling Urutia's discharge indefinitely until he was well enough to return to Spain. Some months later as the situation for Jews had become more and more intolerable and thousands were taken to concentration camps, such as Buchenwald and Dachau, it was a grateful Urutia who arranged with his own government for immigration visas for myself and my family. As it happened, we did not need to use them, though we greatly appreciated his gesture of friendship.'

However, as Guttmann quickly discovered, in addition to certain privileges his position as Medical Director of the Jewish Hospital also carried awesome responsibilities. One day in the late autumn of 1938 he was telephoned by the Secretary of the Nazi Health Authority. As Medical Director and Chairman of the Jewish Medical Association, Guttmann was told to appear before the Nazi Health Authority at 9 a.m. the following day. He had no choice but to inform his executive committee and present himself. The reason he had been summoned was immediately made plain. He was told that a total of fourteen places had been allocated to Jewish Krankenbehandler to care for the total number of Jewish patients in Breslau and the whole province of Silesia.*

* It is interesting to note that the Jewish population of the whole of Silesia began to decline quite early on in the twentieth century. In 1920 it was approximately 44,000; by 1933 it had dropped to 34,000. After the rise of Nazism, the Jewish community appealed to the League of Nations for aid against the increasing restrictions of their civil rights. From 1933 the rate of

As the Medical Officer ultimately responsible for the wellbeing of these citizens, Guttmann had the temerity – and the guts – to stand up to the Secretary of the Health Office. Risking everything, including his own life, he protested vehemently:

'I refused to accept the allocation of only fourteen places to cope with the treatment and care of Jewish patients, not only in the Jewish Hospital and its associated homes for old people, but also in the whole Jewish community of Breslau, by now reduced to twenty-one thousand people, and in addition the Jewish communities of other Silesian towns. I reminded the Secretary that these absurd new arrangements would make any proper medical care of the Jewish population, let alone the running of the hospital, an absolute farce. They were also quite contrary to Hitler's own public statement that the Jewish Hospitals in Germany should not be interfered with in their functions and in their care for Jews – at least not for the time being. Moreover, I explained that, by order of the Health Authorities, all Jewish patients in the provincial mental hospitals had to be transferred to the neurological department of our hospital, which would only add to the work which had to be done. It would be quite impossible to keep the hospital functioning.'

The secretary, unaware of the magnitude of the problem and no doubt impressed by Guttmann's passionate arguments, agreed to listen. After long discussions, a compromise was reached: a minimum of eighty-four practitioners and specialists were to be allowed out of the existing three hundred Jewish doctors in place of the fourteen originally offered. Guttmann also specified that priority appointments should be given to ex-service medical officers from the First

emigration accelerated rapidly and by 1939 the number of Jews remaining in Silesia was 15,480, most of whom perished.

World War, which would ensure a group of experienced doctors and surgeons. If any of these doctors emigrated or retired, their places were to be filled. On the whole, Guttmann was satisfied:

'I left the Secretary's office at 1 p.m. very tired but somewhat relieved. The Secretary kept his word and, to my surprise, these eighty-four places for the medical care of Jewish patients were agreed by the Board of the Health Council, in spite of objections, as I was informed by the Secretary later, by the Nazi Reich's Medical Council in Berlin.

'I had now the invidious and unhappy task to explain the serious, although somewhat improved, situation at an emergency meeting of the Jewish Medical Association. I was of course fully aware of the understandable disappointment and misgivings of many colleagues who would not be among the allocation allowed. However, at that meeting, after I had given my detailed report, I was relieved to find great understanding amongst the vast majority of the members of the difficulties which had faced me in these unhappy circumstances. Instead of any criticism on the part of those doctors and surgeons not included in the list of those to continue their practice, to my surprise Dr Bach, a respected senior colleague and not included in the list of eighty-four, proposed a vote of thanks which was followed by a standing ovation. This moving reaction – I had difficulty in concealing my emotion – demonstrated the courage and the understanding of the precarious situation by the members of the Jewish Medical Association.'

The following month, November 1938, saw the relentless persecution of the Jews by the Nazis culminate in infamy: the never-to-be-forgotten Kristallnacht, the Night of Broken Glass. The ostensible precipitating cause was the shooting of a German diplomat in Paris, Ernst von Rath, by a young

Jew, Herschel Grynszpan. His death was seized upon as evidence of a wide-ranging international Jewish conspiracy against Germany. It was the chance that Nazi party leaders had been waiting for, and they took it.

In Breslau the Jewish community watched fearfully and waited: 'We knew that it would blow up – and it did.' During that night of 9/10 November, in a nationally organised pogrom of devastating efficiency, Jewish synagogues, cemeteries, shops, schools, homes and businesses were ravaged. Ninety-one people were killed. The cost in damage to property amounted to millions. Breslau was not spared:

'I was informed in the morning of the 9th that the fine, large, seventy-year-old building of the main synagogue in Breslau of the Liberal Congregation was burning. Incredulous of such sacrilege, I rushed to the scene to find a huge crowd watching in silence as the synagogue became enveloped in flames and smoke. Men in SS uniform played football with prayer books in the forecourt in the presence of Dr Reinhold Lewin, who just three days before was introduced as the new Chief Rabbi of the Congregation. I left the scene sick at heart and deeply shocked.

'Some thirty thousand Jews were arrested in Germany and most of them dragged off to concentration camps; many were beaten up or tortured and some murdered. In Breslau, many hundreds were arrested indiscriminately and thrown into concentration camps, regardless of their age. On arrival in Buchenwald, some of the older ones who could not get out quickly enough from the cattle trucks in which they were transported were beaten up. Arriving at their barracks they were given a spicy soup, causing diarrhoea. One can imagine the conditions of the victims who had to use the latrines in the cold weather without adequate cleansing material. In the morning the prisoners, their heads shaven –

an automatic procedure – had to assemble outside their barracks and stand for hours on parade in the cold weather.

'Naturally, some of the older men could not stand that "treatment" and developed pneumonia or heart atacks from which they died. Amongst these was one of my close friends, Ismar Neustadt, a well-known industrialist in Breslau who, with his brother, was renowned for great charitable work. Ismar was sixty-three years old and in poor health when taken to Buchenwald, where he died within a few weeks. The first news his widow received of Ismar's death was when she received his ashes, brought to her house by an SS man.'

Kristallnacht was the prelude to the Holocaust of the early 1940s, killing millions of Jewish men, women and children. Those who were spared incarceration or worse in November 1938 found life increasingly difficult. Some, Guttmann remembered, 'found refuge with Christian friends, others constantly changed their places of residence to escape concentration camps. Gradually, victims of these camps – the majority of those from Breslau were taken to Buchenwald and Sachsenhausen – returned with shaven heads, looking like criminals, with frostbitten toes or fingers and other physical as well as mental disturbances, and were admitted to our hospital. One had to see for oneself the physical condition and misery of these victims to realise the whole tragedy. It was little consolation on that day, 10 November 1938, to be rung up at home and at the hospital by many Gentile friends and former patients, and even strangers, expressing utter bewilderment at this terror.'

During that night of savagery, Guttmann, as Medical Director of the Jewish Hospital, gave orders that any male person should be admitted without question; he was determined that the hospital should also serve as a place of refuge. Sixty-four men were admitted. The situation could hardly have been more grim. He remembered it with terror:

'On 10 November, the hospital was occupied by an action group of Gestapo and SS officers and I was rung up by the lay administrator to come immediately, as he added in a trembling voice: "The gentlemen are here." My first reaction was fear of impending death. Aware that I would be the first to be taken to a concentration camp, I put my warmest overcoat on and left my home. I had said goodbye to my wife and my children, who were still asleep. A short distance from the hospital I realised I had on light shoes – summer shoes. The simple thought: "You cannot go to a concentration camp without winter boots" restored my self-control. I returned home – much to Else's short-lived delight – and changed my shoes. Arriving at the main entrance of the hospital, I was stopped by two SS men brandishing guns. When I told them firmly: "I am the Medical Director of the hospital. Will you let me in at once," something extraordinary happened: they sprang immediately to attention, showing their ingrained obedience to authority!

'The main room of the administration was crowded with medical consultants as well as senior and junior staff, while in the adjacent open office of the Chairman of the Board, two SS officers were sitting with their revolvers on the desk. One of the Gestapo officers "greeted" me abruptly with "Heil Hitler." "I understand," he shouted, "that you gave the instruction to admit any male Jew, and that the large number of sixty-four have been admitted since last night. How do you explain this?" I retorted firmly that the answer was quite simple. Any infirmity or latent physical abnormality could acutely worsen under severe stress, and undoubtedly this was the case following the events of yesterday. With a sneer he ordered: "No, no, you personally will demonstrate every person admitted." I replied that this would be quite impossible unless I was allowed to discuss

75

every case first with the doctor on duty who was responsible for the admission. This was grudgingly granted.

'To my, and my patients' luck, an elderly man was brought in on a stretcher, semi-conscious and groaning and suffering from a stroke, with right-sided hemiplegia. I lifted his paralysed arm, which on release fell back lifelessly. I said to the Gestapo officer: "I take it you are satisfied that this man was a case of emergency admission." In a completely different tone and clearly somewhat alarmed by the patient's obvious condition, his reaction was: "Take him away, take him away."

'From this moment on, I demonstrated to him every case as I would have done at a medical meeting, often inventing ad hoc diagnoses (pulling faces at the terrified "patients" to gain their co-operation). During the following hours we succeeded in saving sixty out of the sixty-four admissions from being taken to a concentration camp. The hospital administrator was also spared from being taken away, by my insistance that without him the whole administration of the hospital would be impossible. After these demonstrations, the Gestapo officer asked me to accompany him through all the wards of the hospital to find out how many Jews were hidden there. The only person discovered hiding was the Chief of the Ophthalmology Department, who was found in the X-ray department. At the Gestapo officer's question as to what he was doing there, he replied "I am waiting for an X-ray." "That you can do in the concentration camp" was the answer, and he and a number of consultants as well as younger medical officers were taken away.

'I myself was told, in the presence of the two SS officers: "You will stay here for the time being and will report every day to me. You are responsible with your head that nothing irregular happens here in the hospital. Verstehen Sie, Herr Doktor?" "Yes, perfectly" was my blunt reply.'

When the Gestapo had finally left the hospital, Guttmann, furiously angry, determined to report the incident to the Nazi Health Authority. Against the advice of his medical colleagues, he did so. Somewhat to his surprise, the Chairman of the Health Authority saw him immediately. He was astonished, and even sympathetic, explaining to Guttmann that the Gestapo action was quite unauthorised. He gave his word that he would look into the matter. He did:

'He kept his promise, and four days later I was summoned to his office and he showed me a letter signed by Himmler that "Die Judenbehandler who were taken to Buchenwald should be discharged." I immediately informed their relatives, but as the weeks went by and no one returned we became more and more despondent. The head of the Department of General Medicine was the first to arrive back. He was in a deplorable physical condition, suffering from intestinal infection. He had lost several stone in weight and was admitted as an in-patient. Gradually one after the other returned, several of them needing in-patient treatment for their physical condition and, frequently and understandably, for their abnormal mental condition. Amongst them was my youngest colleague, who had also been beaten up by Brownshirts on his way to the hospital. He was in an obviously acutely distressed state, and I admitted him at once to the Neurological Department. During the night he tried to commit suicide, but this was fortunately prevented.'

On the grim evening of the Gestapo raid on the hospital, Guttmann was rung by a colleague in Prague, asking him to assist at an operation. His passport, naturally, had been confiscated, but after many official prevarications he was given permission to leave the country. He arrived in Prague with his instruments and found a patient with a cerebellar tumour. This was to be the last brain operation Guttmann performed in Europe.

Some weeks later came an incident which was both comic and tragic. In December 1938, Guttmann received a telegram from his friend Dr Almeida Dias, a neuro-pathologist in Lisbon, asking him to come to Lisbon immediately as he had developed paraplegia. Guttmann was then informed by his hospital administrator that the Portuguese Department of the Foreign Office had telephoned to find out whether or not he was in a concentration camp. On learning that he was not, he was told that Dr Salazar, dictator of Portugal, had been personally in touch with Ribbentrop to find out whether Guttmann was available to operate on a sick friend:

'A few minutes later, I was rung up by the Chief of the Portuguese Department of the German Foreign Office, asking whether I would be prepared to fly immediately to see the patient, Dias. When I told him that my passport was still with the Gestapo, he replied "Please go there and it will be handed over to you, including a certificate of political clearance," the latter being required by the Franco–Spanish Government. It was indeed a fantastic situation that the Nazi Government should ask a Jewish neurosurgeon, whose licence as a member of the medical profession had been withdrawn only a few months earlier, to go abroad on an official mission to oblige the Portuguese Government, with whom the Nazis were most anxious to maintain friendly relations.'

In Lisbon Guttmann was met by several professors, one of whom exclaimed: 'Thank God we got you out of a concentration camp.' Guttman was able to lift his hat and reply, 'As you can see, I am still unshaven.' He found his patient, Dr Dias, much improved, and decided not to operate. However, he stayed on for some days, during which time he was offered several top medical positions. He declined these, because he had already received a tentative offer from the British Society for the Protection of Science and Learning, with whom he had been secretly in touch for some time and on whom he had pinned his hopes.

On his return to Germany, having at last made the decision that the political situation was untenable, Guttmann applied for and received a visa allowing him to travel to London for three days. His visit was successful. Many years later he wrote, joyously, of that time:

'At the office of the Society for the Protection of Science and Learning I was told that the visas for me and my family were already at the Embassy in Berlin, which gave me a feeling of tremendous relief. So I sent a terse cable to my wife – "Start packing."'

Guttmann's colleagues at the Jewish Hospital showed full understanding; many were themselves about to emigrate. To the end, by then only a matter of weeks away, Guttmann remained absorbed in his work, so Else began the sad negotiations with tax and emigration officials. Finally, the family was allowed to take with them a minimum of furniture, books, certain surgical instruments and some clothing. The artificially high tax imposed on those items was such that little money was left. What there was was handed over to Ludwig's father, Bernhard, who was staying behind. Even so, the Nazis left nothing to chance. All packing crates had to be inspected by a customs officer. Guttmann related his last – and extraordinarily humane – personal experience of the Nazi Reich:

'On 8 March 1939, the day designated for supervising the packing of our baggage and crate, a Customs officer arrived at 9 a.m., introducing himself with the unusual greeting of "Good morning" instead of "Heil Hitler." "My name is Bayer," he said, "and I have to supervise the packing of your baggage." He then asked whether he could see me alone in my consulting room, the contents of which were the last to be removed. There he told me how deep was his and his senior colleagues' sorrow about the Nazi atrocities, and how all in his department regretted that we had to leave Germany. He explained to me that he and his family had always been treated by a Jewish doctor until this was forbidden by law. He himself was suffering from a painful disorder of his spine following an accident, and to my utter astonishment he asked me whether I would do him the favour of examining him. When, being suspicious that his request was a trap, I asked him whether he was aware that it was a "crime" against the law to consult a Jewish doctor in 1939 he answered: "But I trust you will help me and not report me." Reluctantly, I examined him and gave him advice. He proved his gratitude by going to the packing room, just introducing himself to the workers and immediately leaving the room again, sitting in my office the whole day without supervising the work.

'In the early afternoon his superior officer arrived, who immediately also expressed his warm sympathy with us. Told by Bayer that everything was in order, he did not even bother to go to the room where the workers were still finishing packing, and left after a cup of coffee. When the packing was finished, Bayer told me he had to go to another family, but would return in the early morning with another colleague to seal up the open boxes himself, so that his colleague would only supervise the transfer of the baggage into the crate. He also mentioned that he should now officially ask for the key of the flat – we had arranged to stay with a friend overnight – but he declined to accept the doorkey, obviously disregarding his duty. This gesture was, of course, a clear hint to me to use the opportunity to smuggle money, jewellery etc. into the unsealed boxes. However, still somewhat suspicious about the whole affair, and thinking it could be a trick, we just left.

'Next morning Bayer arrived punctually with a young official, and himself sealed all the boxes and suitcases, so that his colleague only had to supervise their transfer to the crate. When saying goodbye in the corridor, tears were running from his eyes. I tell this story to show that by no means all Germans were Nazis, but many were forced to submit to the inevitable and join the party.'

The Guttmanns left Germany at the French border, at Colmar near Freiberg, the city where Ludwig had spent his carefree student years, where Else had grown up, and where her parents were buried. Her daughter Eva, then a little girl, still remembers her mother crying bitterly. They were leaving behind their home, their friends and close members of their family, to what fate they dared not imagine. On that cheerless day, in that bitter situation, they were the lucky ones.

England
and the War Years

◆◆◆

THE GUTTMANNS came to England via Paris where they were met and seen on their way by Dr Urutia, Ambassador of Guatemala to Franco's Spain. The two men had remained in touch, Urutia showing genuine concern for the Guttmanns' safety as the political situation within Germany worsened. Seeing him briefly in Paris at the time of such anguish and uncertainty, Guttmann noted that he had indeed 'proved both a grateful patient *and friend*'. Urutia was then able to pay Guttmann the fees he owed for his medical treatment in Breslau, thus slightly augmenting the family's total capital of forty marks, the ten per person allowed by the Nazi authorities.

By 1939, much had appeared in the world's press about the plight of Jews in Germany since Hitler came to power. Despite pernicious Nazi propaganda, fair-minded people everywhere recognised and abhorred their persecution, and the nationally organised pogrom of Kristallnacht had shocked the world. The British House of Commons immediately passed an all-party motion deploring the outrage and demanding a united international policy to help solve the problem of German Jewish refugees. On 2 January 1939 *The Times* reported, without comment, that no Jew in Germany could henceforth own or drive a car. It was clear that Jews had been reduced to nonentities, almost slaves, in a country where they had believed themselves to be full citizens, and to which they had contributed so much. The confinement of large numbers of Jews in concentration camps was already well documented (although only a few people, Ludwig Guttmann among them, knew the brutality of the conditions under which they were held). But the concept of what was to become the 'final solution' was still beyond the imaginings of civilised people in the middle of the twentieth century.

The problem of re-settlement, however, seemed intractable: where could the more than half a million Jews rejected by Nazi Germany now live? As more facts concerning their treatment became known, there was genuine sympathy for Jews in Germany, but even in the two countries most willing to accept them, the United States and Great Britain, there were grave difficulties. In the UK, unemployment was high throughout the 1930s; two million in 1939, some twelve per cent of the insured workforce; there was a realistic fear of too great an influx of refugees increasing unemployment and competing for jobs, a wariness which permeated all walks of life. The British Medical Association, for example, adamantly refused to admit more than a limited number of refugee doctors who might wish to practise in this country. Nevertheless, the Home Office estimated that during the years 1933–49 approximately twenty-nine thousand German Jews were settled permanently in this country, including children sent out of Germany alone by their desperate parents. Almost all of these refugees were sponsored by voluntary organisations like the Lord Baldwin Fund and various Jewish Aid committees. But funds on their behalf were also being collected from such diverse sources as Rotary Clubs, the proceeds of a nativity play in Forest Row in Sussex, and of the jobs undertaken by Girl Guides.

When the Guttmanns left Germany their son Dennis was eight and their daughter Eva four. Neither can recall much of that fateful journey, which must have seemed to them quite inexplicable. Eva has a single, vivid childhood memory of being taken to see the synagogue they attended in Breslau after it had been burnt and partly destroyed by the Nazis. On that cold March day of 1939, despite even the immigration officer's kindness, she had caught a proverbial English cold, and she and her mother stayed with friends in London for a few days. Ludwig and Dennis went straight to Oxford, where the family spent some weeks in the Master's Lodge at Balliol College as guests of Mr and Mrs A.D. Lindsay, while they looked for a home of their own. When they arrived in Oxford, the two Guttmanns were met at the station by Professor Francis Simon, former Professor of Physics at Breslau Technical University. He had left Breslau earlier to become Professor Lindemann's (later Lord Cherwell) associate at the Clarendon Laboratory. In the car, driving to Balliol, Guttmann asked him, somewhat hesitantly, how he found life in Oxford. He received this encouraging reply: 'It varies, naturally, but Oxford has one great disadvantage – once you are here, you never want to leave!'

Genuinely grateful to the Lindsays for their hospitality and tactful guidance, the Guttmanns were soon settled in a tiny semi-detached – 63 Lonsdale Road in Summertown. It was a far cry from the roomy, well-ordered apartment in Breslau; three up, two down, with a kitchen containing a coal-fired boiler and a scullery with a sink. Else had to grapple with open fires downstairs and a paraffin heater upstairs. Eva remembers awful chilblains every winter. The too-large furniture, which Else had arranged to have shipped over, was a poignant reminder of their former affluent life. But she was a natural home-maker and provided the domestic stability which enabled the family to survive the shattering dislocation of leaving Germany.

The children started school at Greycoates, a preparatory school; the headmistress waived the fees, since she knew the

Guttmanns could not afford to pay for private education. During the first strange weeks and months in their new country, the whole family experienced one common problem, language. In spite of initial obstinacy on Eva's part, both children were speaking fluent English within three months; an understanding of the grammar took longer. Their parents, on the brink of middle age, found English much harder to acquire and Guttmann retained quite a heavy German accent for the rest of his life. (An amusing boast of his was that once, giving a medical paper, he was mistaken by one of the audience for a Yorkshireman.)

For both Ludwig and Else Guttmann, struggling to establish a new life for themselves and their children, their hesitant speech was deeply frustrating. Guttmann, who claimed he had never shown much aptitude for modern languages even at school, now found it almost impossible, at forty, to learn the use of colloquial English. He was enormously relieved when, after living in England for two-and-a-half years, he recalled having his first dream in *English*. However, overcoming this language barrier had, he felt, one important bearing on his work as a practising neurologist:

'The difficulty in finding the correct expression was really tantalising, and at some stage I behaved in a similar fashion to a motor aphasic, that is I knew what I wanted to say but was unable to find the proper words. It became more than ever abundantly clear to me how tormenting it must be for people with partial motor aphasia following a stroke to express themselves properly. This led me to a better understanding of their sometimes emotional reactions as a result of speech defects ... and an increased admiration for the patience of speech therapists who have to deal with the emotional upsets of such patients.'

Guttmann began work, almost immediately, as Research Fellow at the Nuffield Department of Neurosurgery in the

Radcliffe Infirmary, under Professor Hugh Cairns, a pioneer in neurosurgery in this country. Guttmann remembered Cairns as a 'tough Australian. He and his associate, Joe Pennybaker, a tall, slender and good-looking American from Tennessee, were most kind and helpful to me. For some time I shared Joe's room until a room in the "Rotunda" of the Radcliffe Infirmary was made available for my studies.' Guttmann continued his research on the neuro-regulation of sweat glands, and was also engaged in animal experimental work on nerve regeneration at the Department of Zoology and Comparative Anatomy with J. Z. Young (who later became Professor of Anatomy at University College, London) and Peter Medawar, a 1960 Nobel prize winner for his work on tissue transplantation. Later Guttmann became interested in peripheral nerve physiology, nerve suture and galvanic exercise of denervated muscles following nerve injuries. This aspect of his work became especially important during the war, for the investigation and treatment of peripheral nerve injuries.

In addition to his research at the Radcliffe Infirmary, Guttmann also became a member of the Senior Common Room at Balliol. He received small grants from the Society for the Protection of Science and Learning, and from Balliol, which amounted to £200 a year, later increased to £300. Since they had brought with them only some personal possessions, the family's circumstances were indeed straitened. With typical candour, Guttmann admitted to an interviewer, much later, that the family had had a hard time making ends meet during their early years in this country.

Of two children, Eva, four years the younger, was the most disturbed by the upheaval. While she was still confused by the language and had not yet made friends with other children in the street she remembers to this day bursting into tears almost continually, and her father nicknamed her the German equivalent of 'weeping Lizzie'. In due course Dennis Guttmann, through the kind intervention of the wife of a senior don at Balliol, entered the famous Dragon School, where he was given an assisted place. Eventually the children, as healthy children will, grasped their new language, made friends and flourished.

Consequently it was upon Else Guttmann that the burden of the family's refugee status fell most heavily. Suddenly, she was deprived of her comfortable home in Breslau, servants, and a full social life. She was deeply worried for the safety of her two sisters, to whom she had been extremely close. (One had already left Germany for the United States; the other had disappeared with her children into a concentration camp.) She was still wrestling with a foreign language and, to some extent, a culture and customs which were alien to her. While her husband was carrying out an aspect of the work to which he was completely dedicated and her children were in school, Else Guttmann was extremely short of money and more or less confined to the house. But the strength and resourcefulness for which her children remember her so affectionately did not desert her. Eva remembers waking in the night to see her mother sitting at her sewing machine, making wax cloth shopping bags, thereby providing a small but valuable contribution to the family's depleted budget. Later, when Dennis went to boarding school, Else let his room to lodgers, the last of them being Max Beloff (later Lord Beloff). However, despite emotional anguish, there were compensations of which the two adult members of the family, at least, were deeply aware. Above all, after years of danger and distrust, they had achieved personal safety in a tolerant and democratic society.

It was a time of uncertainty and upheaval throughout Europe. As though in anticipation of the holocaust, in his New Year sermon the Archbishop of Canterbury had asked his congregation, despairingly, 'Are there not signs of a return to the Dark Ages?' On 15 March 1939 (the day after the Guttmanns reached Dover) Hitler's infantry poured through the streets of Prague; Germany had occupied Czechoslovakia. Hope for Prime Minister Chamberlain's policy of appeasement, 'Peace with Honour', was fading. Throughout Britain talk of another war, just twenty years after the Armistice had been signed, became a national pastime. The Allies' response to Hitler's aggression in Czechoslovakia was yet another ominous step in that direction. In the House of Commons, Anthony Eden, Chamberlain's former Foreign Secretary, pronounced: 'We are heading for a universal tragedy which is going to engulf us all.'

Meanwhile, Ludwig Guttmann was discovering that Oxford was no longer the legendary dreaming university and market town he had imagined: 'It was greatly transformed by Lord Nuffield's industrial empire. Yet wandering through the beautiful quadrangles and gardens of the ancient colleges, Oxford still seemed to me to have retained its unique character and tradition.' Because of his position at Balliol and the reputation he had acquired in medical circles from his years with Foerster, Guttmann met the leading figures of the university: in addition to his original host, Dr Lindsay (later Lord Lindsay), the professors Gilbert Murray, C. M. Bowra and F. A. Lindemann. He found these eminent men deeply concerned with the plight of oppressed people: 'They had realised very early the evil of Hitler's Nazi regime. They were not bluffed by the lies and promises of the Nazis as many people in England and other countries had been. This group was strongly opposed to the form of Fascism which had developed in the 1930s under the leadership of Oswald Mosley and his "Blackshirts," and had made some impression in England.'

Guttmann describes a revealing interview he had with Professor Lindemann in the spring of 1939, when he was invited to meet him soon after his arrival in England: 'F. A. Lindemann was then Professor of Experimental Philosophy and Head of the Clarendon Laboratory for Physics. He had built up this department to one of international repute. He had made his name in the First World War as a research pilot by introducing, after cold-blooded, courageous flying experiments, his spiral-spin technique which gave aeronautics a new military manoeuvre. He was a close friend and adviser of Churchill, deeply involved in politics and belonging to the group of professors who hated the Nazi regime. Our conversation was conducted in German, as my English at that time was hopelessly inadequate, and he, being born in Germany – his family came from Alsace – spoke German fluently. He asked me about the political situation there. I explained to him the reasons why, as Medical Director of the Jewish Hospital, I had felt it my duty to stay as long as possible. We discussed, in general terms, the re-armament of the German forces and I told him of the profound disappointment of thousands of Germans when Britain and France stood by when Hitler re-occupied the Rhineland ... then Czechoslovakia.

'When I asked him whether he would like to know about events of my personal experience he was very anxious to learn. However, when I told him of the burning of books, the condition of people admitted to my hospital after interrogation by the Gestapo, broken in body and spirit, and of the events of the Kristallnacht, he somewhat sneeringly interrupted me, saying "You must not tell me atrocity legends." I became hot under my collar and sharply replied: "Sir, these are not legends, these are facts I have witnessed with my own eyes," whereupon he immediately apologised, exclaiming "But these horrible things are beyond the comprehension of a normal person!" I replied that I could well understand his reaction, because in 1933 I had felt as incredulous as he was now, but I had had subsequently to live and work for almost six years under these appalling conditions. He suddenly turned purple, clenched his fists, shook his arms and shouted "This man Chamberlain must go!" This outburst made to me, a stranger, naturally was somewhat embarrassing but obviously in line with Lindemann's tough character.'

Although Guttmann's research at the Radcliffe was far removed from his previous clinical work and responsibilities in Breslau, he realised how fortunate he was to have it. He counted his blessings, foreswore bitterness, and got on with the job with characteristic vigour. As he acknowledged later, 'I did not experience, as many of my fellow refugees did – doctors, lawyers and members of other professions – that enforced inactivity which, resulting in frustration and apathy, had disastrous mental and physical effects on some of them.' All refugees in Great Britain had to be vetted by a tribunal with regard to their reliability. Both Else and Ludwig Guttmann were graded C – reliable; and Guttmann was not interned, as were many refugees, whatever their status, after the collapse of France in 1940.

Through the summer of 1939, war seemed more and more inevitable. Most people accepted that it was simply a question of time, yet ordinary life continued. The new King and Queen, George VI and Queen Elizabeth, made a triumphant tour of Canada and the United States. A popular car sticker bore the slogan 'Half a mo, Hitler, let's have our holidays first.' It was on 3 September that Chamberlain finally broadcast to the nation '... this country is now at war with Germany ...'

Mindful as he must have been of the terrible irony of his situation – and of thousands like him – Ludwig Guttmann went at once to his superior, Dr Hugh Cairns, and offered his services to the armed forces. They were refused. Although Guttmann pointed out vehemently that his previous experience would be most valuable in treating war injuries, Cairns nevertheless advised him to continue his experimental research work on nerve regeneration, which he felt was essential to the war effort. At that time, also, Guttmann was involved in the plans for setting up a Centre for Peripheral Nerve Injuries at the Orthopaedic Wingfield-Morris Hospital in Oxford. With the greatest reluctance he acceded to Cairns' advice, though he believed later that his availability in 1943, when the new spinal injuries unit at Stoke Mandeville was first planned, was indeed providential.

Meanwhile, the home front braced itself for the onslaught ... but for month after month there was an eerie silence – the 'phony' war when nothing much seemed to be happening so far as civilians were concerned. This phase of the war ended abruptly in September 1940 when the first Luftwaffe planes appeared out of a cloudless sky over London. Oxford, like Cambridge, was spared the bombing and settled down to a relatively quiet war; the dreary round of blackout, queueing and shortages. Streams of evacuees seeking respite from heavily bombed areas came and went, swelling the town's population.

Although hard, those years of the war were happy ones for the Guttmanns. The family got used to sleeping under the stairs on mattresses in case of air raids and taking gas masks everywhere. They all had bicycles, although Guttmann never mastered the art and gave up after riding straight into a wall. There was always enough to eat in spite of rationing and Else was a resourceful cook, augmenting their diet with home-grown vegetables from their small back

91

garden, which she had dug and planted with great success. She was an enthusiastic and expert gardener for the rest of her life.

The Jewish community of Oxford had increased in numbers dramatically because of so many refugees fleeing from the Nazis and also from the bombs in London. Else quickly became a leading spirit in running a centre for Jewish refugees where they could meet, speak in their own language and eat a kosher meal. She also took part in setting up a group of the Women's International Zionist Organisation in Oxford and became chairman.

There were always people in and out of 163 Lonsdale Road. Everyone was warmly welcomed, particularly on Jewish festivals such as Passover, the New Year and Chanukah. The small sitting/dining-room was crammed full with family and guests enjoying the meals superbly prepared and lovingly served by Else – with Ludwig an excellent and lively host. Although they did not maintain a kosher home, the Guttmanns were meticulous in maintaining Jewish family traditions.

Guttmann became an air raid warden in the street where they lived: 'One night, I rushed out on duty as the sirens wailed, to be joined by other members of the team. Realising that I was by far the youngest, I could not help admiring the old ladies of between sixty and seventy who carried their stirrup pumps with grim determination, ready to tackle bombs and fire. God knows what would have happened had they ever had to use them!'

As the years dragged on, even Ludwig Guttmann's zest for his research started to flag. With the war effort demanding the most of every man and woman in the country, he was increasingly despondent at being kept away from clinical work. He was convinced that he could have been more usefully employed in the immediate treatment of war casualties with injuries to the nervous system, at first aid stations or base hospitals. At no time during those years from 1939 to 1943, a period of severe national crisis, was any such opportunity offered to him. He began seriously to consider studying for a medical degree which would enable him to register as a general practitioner in the UK. But it was also during this frustrating professional hiatus that he wrote two influential surveys which profoundly affected his later career.

In 1941, Dr George Riddoch, then the leading neurologist of The London Hospital, asked Guttmann to submit reviews to the Peripheral Nerve Committee of the Research Council, of which he was chairman: first, on the surgical aspects of spinal injuries and secondly, on rehabilitation after injuries to the nervous system. Guttmann believed that it was these surveys, the culmination of his previous wide experience in Germany, which enabled him to formulate 'a fundamentally different philosophy and concept of the management of spinal cord sufferers. This was at variance with the attitudes of centuries, which, even during the Second World War, still prevailed towards these unfortunate victims of war and peace.'

These reviews (neither of which exists today in its original form) were well received, particularly by Dr Riddoch, then a Brigadier General, and he took note of Ludwig Guttmann, refugee and medical outsider. It is to Riddoch that credit must go for recognising, as other figures of the medical establishment did not, Guttmann's potential, and the tragic waste of his abilities in the field of pure research.

Guttmann continues the story:

'In September 1943 Dr Riddoch asked to see me in his office in Oxford – the headquarters of neurology and neurosurgery. He knew me very well by this time. He said to me: "Look here, we know your views about paraplegics, which are pretty radical, but we have to open another spinal unit as one of the preparations for the second front, which will start next spring. I know you are pretty fed up with all the research ... Would you like to do it?" I said: "*Yes. Is it today or tomorrow?!*" But I told him that I was still not naturalised – and that I must have a free hand to find out whether my philosophy could be put into practice. *And it was granted.*

'There were two possible hospitals, one in Basingstoke and one in Stoke Mandeville. I saw the one in Stoke Mandeville, which seemed suitable as it was built on the ground floor with wide corridors and so on. But, of course, the facilities were practically non-existent. It was an uphill fight. The story of the Spinal Injuries Unit of Stoke Mandeville, and my specialisation in the complex problems of this long neglected area of medicine, is difficult to tell dispassionately. It demanded the "blood, sweat and tears" not uncommonly found in pioneer work ... *I lived at its very core.*'

Stoke Mandeville

———◆◆———

DESPITE LUDWIG GUTTMANN'S ELATION at his new appointment – and the prospect of again working with patients after
four years of research – many of his colleagues were surprised
at his enthusiasm for the daunting task he had so who-
leheartedly undertaken: 'They could not understand how I
could leave Oxford University to be engulfed in the hopeless
and depressing task of looking after traumatic spinal paraplegics, let alone tetraplegics.'

Today, it is difficult for us to comprehend the ingrained
attitudes of hopelessness towards disabled people which
existed in 1944 – and, in all too frequent instances, for many
years thereafter. (A medical student in a London teaching
hospital in the 1950s, now a consultant physician, still
remembers a paraplegic patient confined to a corner of the
ward, dying of septic sores.) Yet without such comprehension, the world-wide impact of the work done at Stoke
Mandeville, instigated and inspired by Ludwig Guttmann,
cannot be properly evaluated.

'Nowadays,' Guttmann wrote in 1980, shortly before his
death, 'in view of the dramatic changes which have been
made in this subject of injuries of the spinal cord, one is
inclined to forget the helplessness of generations of physicians and surgeons when faced with the management of
these patients.' He was fond of quoting an Egyptian papyrus
of the second millenium BC, which described spinal cord

damage as '*a condition not to be treated*'. Essentially, in the winter of 1943–44, similar attitudes prevailed both in the medical profession and in society at large.

Throughout history, paraplegia had been considered one of the greatest tragedies to beset mankind. At that time, towards the end of the Second World War, Guttmann considered it to be 'the most depressing and neglected subject of all medicine'. He explained:

'It must be remembered that the spinal cord, that big nerve trunk within the vertebral column, is one of the most important organs in animals and man. For it is the main mediator of all impulses from and to the brain. For instance, any volitional isolated muscle movement initiated from the brain is only possible if the spinal cord is intact and vice versa – all forms of sensory impulses originating from the skin, muscles, joints and internal organs have to travel through the spinal cord to be consciously appreciated. Moreover, in addition to these vital functions the cord contains in itself nerve centres for controlling bladder, bowels, sexual and respiratory functions.

'Therefore if the spinal cord is severed or crushed – by a knife, bullet, vascular catastrophe (thrombosis) or by a fracture of the spine at any level – this immediately results in a paralysis *below* the level of the injury, with loss of most essential functions. This involves all voluntary motor functions, appreciation of all forms of sensation, and results in loss of posture and control of bladder and bowels. Sexual function in men is abolished. Women lose sexual sensation but can have intercourse and still conceive. The higher up the spine the level of the injury the more parts of the body are cut off. In injuries of the cervical cord, the respiratory function as well as the blood circulation are greatly impaired, especially in very high cervical lesions, the involvement of the blood circulation leading also to a reduction of the tone of all tissues, especially skin and muscles. This in turn results in a lowering of their resistance to pressure, which is one of the most important causes of the development of pressure sores. All forms of sensation are cut off and the patient does not feel the discomfort of pressure, such as non-paralysed people do in the form, let us say, of pins and needles.

'The victims of war, road, industrial and sporting accidents did not establish a social problem in the past, as their life expectancy was very short, two to three years at the utmost as a rule. Complications such as sepsis from ascending infection of the bladder into the kidneys, and pressure sores, were considered inevitable. Therefore, any attempt to restore such a person to his or her former social activities seemed to be out of the question, and the view generally held was the sooner they died the better for all concerned.'

Like most men and women of his generation, British, European and American, Ludwig Guttmann had been unhappily aware of the plight of spinal cord injured veterans of the First World War. He said that seeing them in hospitals, usually without hope, had left him with 'very depressing memories'. Also close to his own consciousness were the paralysed miners he had seen dying in the Accident Hospital in Königshütte. All the medical literature with which Guttmann was familiar approached the subject of paraplegia with bleakness and foreboding. At the turn of the century, two respected German doctors, Wagner and Stolper, wrote of severe spinal cord injury that 'it is the physician's forlorn task, even while knowing that the patient is approaching an early death, to keep him (or her) alive for weeks and months on end, only to see him wretchedly fade away despite all skill and efforts'. Harvey Cushing, the brilliant American neurosurgeon at Harvard University whom Guttmann had planned to visit in 1929, had been a consultant in neurosurgery to the American Army in the First World War. He wrote of his experiences with spinal cord injured soldiers at the front: 'Conditions were such ... as to make it almost impossible to give the unfortunate men the care their injuries required. No water beds were available and each case demanded the individual attention of a nurse trained in the care of paraplegics. Only those cases survived in which the spinal cord damage was partial.'

The mortality rate of spinal cord injuries in the First World War in the British Army had been equally high: death within the first few weeks or months varied from forty-seven per cent to sixty-five per cent (Vellacott and Webb-Johnson) and the overall mortality after three years was estimated at eighty per cent (Thompson and Walker 1937). Guttmann summed up the outlook for paraplegics as it then was:

'Most of those who managed to survive were doomed to spend the rest of their lives as pensioners at home or in institutions for incurables, dependent on other people's assistance and, as a rule, given no incentive or encouragement to return to a useful life. On the contrary, the existing legislation and regulations regarding war pensions or workmen's compensation made it quite impossible for these totally disabled men (or women) to return to paid employment for fear of losing their pensions or compensation. Indeed, until the Disabled Persons Act (1944) was passed in Britain, society still adhered to the conception of the ancient Greeks, that a hundred per cent disablement excluded the disabled from any possibility of remunerative work.'

Right up to and during the Second World War, therefore, doctors regarded paraplegia with profound pessimism. It is astonishing, now, to read a report of the Medical Council in 1924 which expressed the belief that 'The paraplegic patient may live for a few years in a state of more or less ill health.' And the following is a depressing, but factual, account of the condition in which paraplegics (tetraplegics were not even mentioned) vegetated at a home for disabled ex-servicemen from the 1914–18 war:

'Two or three times a week the patient is bathed. This means he must be lifted from his bed to his ward chair and wheeled into the bathroom where his pyjamas and night-clothes are removed and he is placed in a very warm bath and washed by an orderly ... there is more morphia, atrophine and hyoscine used in this home ... than in any other place of its size in the country.'

Well into the middle years of this century, the majority of disabled men and women of sound mind were consigned to what Guttmann described as 'the human scrapheap'. Only gradually did attitudes start to change. There were many contributory factors – the dedication of doctors such as Ludwig Guttmann, who became an outstanding innovator in the field; antibiotics; the legitimate demands, and the determination of paraplegics themselves.

In the light of what followed, it is important to make mention of the work of Dr D. Monroe at Boston City Hospital in Massachusetts in the early 1940s. Using many of the same techniques which were later tried so successfully at the Spinal Injuries Unit at Stoke Mandeville, Dr Monroe made some practical headway in treating paraplegics and encouraging them to lead independent lives. Monroe's publications on the subject made little impact at that time in the US or the UK; but they should be remembered as milestones pointing the way ahead.

Some evidence of enlightenment in this country came during the Second World War. In an attempt to deal with the complexities of spinal cord afflictions, the medical authorities set up twelve spinal units in various parts of the country to which most of the surviving war casualties with these injuries were sent. These units were attached to different departments – neurological, psychiatric or urological – on the grounds that spinal cord sufferers were best treated together rather than scattered in general wards. Guttmann, however, did not believe this was a satisfactory arrangement because 'the units to which these disabled people were attached could deal only with specific problems and short-term treatment . . . and were unable to give acutely ill patients the detailed care that the subject of spinal paralysis demands day and night'. An independent report later confirmed Guttmann's opinion, acknowledging that 'No one member of a team devoted more than part of his time to the care of spinal injury cases . . .'

Guttmann's own views as to what treatment such a patient required were, as Dr Riddoch knew, far more radical. Never one to mince his words, Guttmann had already stated quite bluntly that 'it was not then realised, either by medical or administrative authorities, that in order to prevent spinal units from becoming merely an accumulation of doomed cripples, the provision of certain basic arrangements was absolutely indispensable . . .'

An early advocate of 'total care', Guttmann believed it essential that each unit had its own experienced physician who was prepared to give up part of his own speciality in order to devote his full time to this complex subject of medicine and surgery; to plan and organise the many details of treatment; and to correlate the sometimes conflicting interests of visiting medical and surgical specialists involved in the immediate or long-term management of paraplegics and tetraplegics. He demanded nurses to give their undivided care day and night to the acutely ill; plus back-up paramedical staff such as physiotherapists, all in adequate numbers. Additionally, research facilities were needed to investigate damage to the spinal cord; arrangements had to be made for domestic and industrial resettlement; and regular after-care check-ups. In short, he envisaged nothing less than a drastically new concept in the treatment of spinal cord sufferers – total care followed by maximum rehabilitation:

'The basic principle of this new philosophy was to provide a comprehensive paraplegia and tetraplegia service to rescue these men, women and children from the human scrapheap and return most of them, in spite of permanent, profound disability – by clinical measures and psychological readjustment – to a life worth living, as useful and respected citizens in the community.'

The opportunity to test these strongly held theories now presented itself. At the age of forty-five, Guttmann found himself in charge of a medical unit for the third time in his life: the first, at Friedrichsberg, when he was twenty-eight; later, at the Jewish Hospital in Breslau; now – Stoke Mandeville. Much in his background and personality had uniquely prepared him for the job ahead, a job perhaps more aptly described as a mission. For Guttmann was a fighter. His passionate sense of justice had been reinforced by his experiences in Nazi Germany. Personal adversity had tested his will and his moral courage. He had a healthy ego. He was forceful – and when he felt himself to be in the right, which was often, he was outspoken and fearless. His wide experience as a neurologist, his research, his many years of work with Foerster and the crucial papers he had prepared for Brigadier General Riddoch had all helped to crystallise his ideas on the management of spinal cord sufferers. Finally, as a foreigner and a medical outsider in Britain, he had nothing to lose, and everything to gain, by attacking an area of medicine which was then considered hopeless and held no appeal for established British surgeons.

There was growing optimism that the war was beginning to be won rather than fought. On the morning of 1 February

101

1944 when the unit opened *The Times* reported: 'The Fifth Army has launched a strong offensive from the Anzio beach-head ... the Russians are advancing closer to the Estonian frontier ... heavy RAF attacks on Berlin ... the total number of bombs dropped there in three nights was five thousand tons ...' Rumours of a second front were everywhere discussed; and it was precisely in sombre anticipation of heavy Allied casualties during landings in Europe that the unit had been planned.

Nevertheless, as he took stock of his new unit – Ward X – on that bleak February night even Ludwig Guttmann's belief in, and enthusiasm for, the job ahead must have been somewhat tempered. After more than four gruelling years of war, people were used to making do and getting on with the job: due to a national shortage of bricks, the hospital was housed in a collection of prefabricated huts. The single ward originally allotted had twenty-six beds. In the early weeks, Guttmann, the newly appointed Director, had no office; his secretary worked in a bathroom off one of the other wards, and the X-ray cabinet was a wooden cupboard laid flat on its back.

His arrival on the scene at Stoke Mandeville was greated without enthusiasm and the unit opened without ceremony: the spinal ward, 'under a German doctor', would certainly mean extra work for hospital staff already under pressure.

As a doctor and a scientist about to embark on a pioneering direction of modern medicine, Guttmann cannot have found the prospects particularly encouraging, yet looking back, he wrote with considerable understatement that 'The medical and paramedical staff delegated to the unit were clearly unprepared and untrained for this purpose. The first nursing staff consisted of Miss W. Merchant, a young state registered sister, commandeered by the Matron to take on the job as sister in charge of the ward. Also, Miss A. Buller, a female auxiliary nurse of motherly type. In addition to the two nurses, eight medical orderlies were seconded from the Army.'

When Guttmann enquired of one of these first orderlies what his medical experience in the Army had been, back came the cheerful answer: 'Shovelling coal, sir ...'! However, Guttmann found that despite their total lack of experience, these strong young orderlies could be satisfactorily trained. Indeed, many became devoted to the work and stayed on for several years after the war. Those who did leave were replaced by medical orderlies from the Polish Army stationed in the UK. And in the early days of the unit, their Director held one persuasive trump card which he did not hesitate to play: slack work would mean dismissal – back to the fighting front.

Guttmann was taken to view his ward by the Medical Superintendent of the hospital and found, as he recalled later, 'thirty *metal* bedpans standing on a shelf like soldiers on parade'. He was appalled. Feigning ignorance, he enquired what they were for. Given the obvious and somewhat patronising answer – 'Surely your patients will be needing them?' – Guttmann exploded, immediately demanding rubber ones instead, 'to prevent pressure sores, not produce them'. Reluctantly, rubber bedpans were obtained. That story is typical of Guttmann's abrasive, but generally successful, skirmishes with bureaucracy. Three days later, the first patient, a wounded soldier called Henry Collier, was admitted to the unit.

Clearly, from those very early confusing days of the Spinal Injuries Unit at Stoke Mandeville, Ludwig Guttmann's first and monumental task was to overcome what he described as 'indoctrinated prejudice', to convince practically everyone – doctors, patients, nurses, administrators, paramedics – that the hard work which he gave, and demanded, was justified:

'The question put to me with almost monotonous regularity was: "Is it all worthwhile?"' This prevailing attitude of defeatism, he realised at once, was the primary obstacle in the way of progress for the disabled. Unless it could be overcome, hopes for returning paraplegic men and women to the community would never be realised. Guttmann therefore set out to prove, as quickly as possible, that the treatment which he had evolved, when strictly carried out, did produce successful results.

The two great dangers that threaten the paraplegic patient are pressure sores and urinary infections. Pressure sores consist of a breakdown of the skin overlying bony prominences and, as they become infected, they may extend deeply enough to cause similar necrosis of the underlying bone. In the healthy person, sitting or lying down in the same position will automatically cause enough discomfort to produce, quite soon, a change of position, but when there is no sensation, these relief movements cannot occur spontaneously.

From the very beginning of his directorship, Guttmann gave the order that all patients at the Spinal Injuries Unit were to be turned prone to supine and back, or from one side to another, every two hours – night and day, waking or sleeping. At first, this aspect of his treatment was greeted sceptically by a staff quick to resent extra heavy work and extremely doubtful of its value. Guttmann resolved the matter in two ways. He began appearing in the ward unexpectedly, at all hours, to make sure that his orders to turn patients and empty urine bottles were being carried out, however unwillingly. In addition, when on his rounds he would use transparent film to trace the shrinking outline of patients' bedsores as they began to heal. He was adamant that only such constant care would allow the sores to heal and prevent the fragile skin from breaking down again. Simple and systematic, the method worked.

He had made his point, practically and encouragingly, both to his staff and to his patients, many of whom had arrived at the unit in an almost putrefying state. 'Turning' became, and has remained, a byword at Stoke Mandeville. Guttmann also established conclusively that all antiseptics *reduced* the rate of healing by damaging epithelial cells – tissue forming the outer layer of the body surface. Only penicillin, then available in limited quantities, helped in certain cases. Guttmann proved very early – to his patients, his staff and his colleagues – that it was his simple but methodical treatment of spinally injured patients that solved the two most serious dangers of bladder infections and pressure sores. Lady (Ethel) Florey, wife of one of its three discoverers, came over from Oxford each week with minute quantities of penicillin, which was then extremely scarce, to be used on skin which had broken down and become septic, and its effects were measured by Lady Florey herself. But Guttmann firmly believed that the effects were marginal; only later did genuinely efficacious antibiotics become available.

Guttmann's understanding of the body tissue's response to pressure also led to his vehement condemnation of plaster beds, then widely used, especially to move spinally injured patients. The appalling condition in which injured servicemen began appearing at Stoke Mandeville convinced Guttmann that although apparently sound in principle, in practice plaster beds did far more harm than good. Within minutes of arrival, Guttmann had the plaster beds in the refuse bin and the patients on pillow packs. Professor David Whitteridge, then a lecturer in physiology at Oxford University, who worked with Guttmann at Stoke Mandeville over the years, recalls:

'One of his many clashes with orthopaedic surgeons occurred at a meeting in 1946 at which I was present, when Guttmann denounced the practice of transporting paraplegics on plaster beds. The principle of spreading the weight of the body so that there were no points of localised pressure was admirable. However, paraplegics, in pain and not eating, wasted so rapidly that they ceased to fit the plaster bed, and arrived at Stoke Mandeville not only with the usual sores over the bones of the pelvis but also with a sore over each vertebral spine, a sight never seen except with plaster beds. Criticism from a civilian was not welcome to the service orthopaedists, but the evidence was incontrovertible.'

As well as the ever-present threat of pressure sores, management of the bladder is a chronic problem for the paralysed. Paraplegics can, of course, no longer void urine voluntarily and repeated catheterisation at regular intervals is particularly incovenient if they are travelling around by car, train or plane; but if it is done with proper aseptic technique (and paraplegics or their attendants can learn this) it carries little risk of infecting the bladder. Previously, it had been standard practice to open the bladder in the midline between the umbilicus and the pubis – called suprapubic cystotomy – and fix a box on the anterior abdominal wall to collect the urine. After weeks or months, the bladder begins to void reflexly, urine may be passed through the natural passage, and with luck the opening on the tummy wall may be closed. This procedure was supposed to reduce the risk of infecting the bladder, which it almost invariably failed to do, and at best patients were left with a small, scarred bladder that emptied reflexly at frequent intervals.

If a patient has to travel far without professional care before reaching a spinal centre, this may still be the only practicable treatment. But Guttmann stressed that immediate catheterisation with strict aseptic precautions, carried out by a doctor and not by an orderly, gave much better results later. All spinally injured patients can now be safely treated without making an opening between the bladder and the lower tummy wall, above the pubic hair line. The major danger for paraplegic patients of urinary infection is of developing an ascending infection with damage to the kidneys. This condition is accompanied by high fever and used to be a major factor in paraplegic mortality rates. Antibiotics can now control the infections, but complete eradication of infection is still only obtained in about seventy per cent of cases.

In the early stages of developing the unit, Guttmann meticulously attended to all the catheters himself. A patient from those days remembers that 'Once he asked me what I felt like after he changed my catheter. I said I felt as though I could kill him. He often reminded me of the incident ...'

It was Ludwig Guttmann's strong belief that operation on the injured spinal cord was, in the vast majority of cases, 'irresponsible meddling'. Surgical intervention at the Spinal Injuries Unit at Stoke Mandeville was therefore rare, because it can cause bruising or bleeding which further damages the spinal cord, usually better left to recover on its own. Guttmann adhered to this belief – too rigidly, some colleagues thought – all his working life, but his judgement was soundly based on the exact knowledge of spinal lesions at every level, which he had meticulously investigated during his years in Germany working with Foerster.

To his staff at Stoke Mandeville, kept on their toes during those first months of the new unit, adjusting to the benign, but absolute, style of the new Director as well as the increasing number of patients, it seemed as though Guttmann literally lived on the job. He did. On his appointment to Stoke Mandeville, Ludwig and Else agreed that their home should remain in Oxford for the time being. Moving house was difficult during war-time and both children were settled in their schools and making good progress; so Guttmann stayed at the hospital and commuted to Oxford whenever he could, often by bus. Later, he bought a car which made the journey easier, although he acquired a reputation for adventurous driving.

Else understood the vital importance of his work to her husband and had appreciated his frustration during the some-times wearisome years of research in Oxford. His position as Director of the Spinal Injuries Unit was entirely suited to his arduous training and the responsible jobs he had held before he emigrated.

Ludwig Guttmann was an intensely hard worker and throughout his life kept long working hours. (Until his health began to fail in old age, he rarely took time off. His son has no recollections of family holidays.) His work absorbed him totally, perhaps even to the detriment of his family life and other interests, such as music, which he had enjoyed in his youth. One positive aspect of Guttmann's new appointment, however, from the family's point of view, was his increase in salary. From the meagre living he had received during his first years in this country, he was now paid on the scale of a senior surgeon. (As it was war-time, the Emergency Medical Services waived his nationality – he was still a German citizen, naturalisation not being possible until after the war – and accepted his medical credentials.) This allowed a more comfortable standard of living, but was still a good deal below that which they had enjoyed in Breslau.

Despite her father's long absences from home, Eva remembers their small house in Oxford as a very happy place at that time of her childhood. Although his single-minded

preoccupation with the Spinal Injuries Unit inevitably produced some friction within the family, Else Guttmann maintained a well-run and loving home which her children still
value. A schoolfriend of Eva's, who knew them all well at
that time, gives a glimpse of quite happy, traditional family
life:

'I was a frequent caller at their house which was semi-
detached, not large, and seemed quite full of one thing or
another. Generally Mrs Guttmann was about, perhaps in the
kitchen, and the house gave an air of purposeful activity.
She kept chickens and we propped our bikes near the coop
where they scratched. Occasionally, I saw Dr Guttmann. He
was rather short and stocky. I can picture him now in his
brown tweed suit. He spoke with a German accent and I
had to listen carefully to understand him. Sometimes he
shouted if things weren't to his liking. Although these mani-
festations were loud and strong I never doubted that they
were a cover for a deep humour, warmth and understanding.
It was his way of getting something done. In spite of his
stoutness, Dr Guttmann moved about briskly. I knew where
I was with him ... On one occasion they took me out to
dinner at The Bear at Woodstock. It was a celebration of
some kind and I was included in the spree. A warm family
feeling prevailed and I felt privileged to be included.'

At Stoke Mandeville, the unit was rapidly filling up with
injured servicemen and civilians who had been wounded on
the home front, largely bombing and fallen masonry. Dr
Paul Jonason was delegated from the Middlesex Hospital to
become Guttmann's first registrar. He settled into the unit
admirably. It is surely a tribute to Ludwig Guttmann's gifts
as a teacher, and to the strength of his personality, that he
was able to exhort and even bully his staff into performing

their jobs the way he wanted. 'In due course,' he said, 'they developed into a first-class team, whose devotion and enthusiasm inspired the patients to become active, and not passive, members of the team.'

One person who quickly became, and remained, an invaluable member of that team was Joan Scruton, Guttmann's first secretary. His description of how she came to work for him, and some of her early duties, gives a vivid picture of the cheerful, makeshift daily routine during the first operating days of the unit:

'The only person who actually and spontaneously volunteered to work with spinal cord sufferers was Joan Scruton, who at that time was in charge of the whole typing pool of the hospital. When I dictated to her the medical notes of my early patients from the war, she felt compassion for the plight of these young soldiers, and when the authorities set up a secretarial post for the unit she applied for the job. She became my secretary.

'One of her first big jobs was to prepare a table of statistics which entailed interviewing every patient in the unit. This plunged her into the unfamiliar routine of ward life to carry out the survey. Amongst the questions of the questionnaire was one: "What are your hobbies?" but of course it is impossible to record some of the answers she received, to her embarrassment, from these young soldiers and officers!'

Given his determination to return paraplegics, wherever possible, to normal life within the community, Guttmann found the training facilities at his disposal depressingly inadequate. At Stoke Mandeville Hospital, as in most other hospitals in Britain and abroad, planned rehabilitation services at that time were in their infancy, and social and industrial rehabilitation of the disabled was carried out, if at all, sporadically. However, the hospital had been built in 1940 as part of the Emergency Medical Services and it did have a workshop, although it was designed only for woodwork: 'In due course by adding shoe repairs, an engraving machine, a drawing-board and a typewriter, this served as pre-vocational training for the patients.'

Guttmann's first instructor, Bill Parker, forged a good working relationship with the Director which lasted until his retirement in 1967: 'He became one of my closest co-workers for many years and with other instructors who were employed afterwards, when the facilities for work-therapy in engineering, draughtsmanship and assembly work were increased, Parker did outstanding work in the training for the industrial resettlement of paraplegics as well as tetraplegics.'

Bill Parker first met Guttmann early in 1944: 'We had not been in conversation very long,' he says, 'when the question of woodwork for paraplegics was brought up. From the first, he was quite clear on his requirements and was definite that all patients of his who were out of bed should be doing some kind of work. Gutmann had only a few patients at that time, but as they were patients of a type I had not worked with before, the method of woodwork instruction and the use of tools at first given was somewhat frightening. However, after some time and with some thought, I was able to overcome the problems which cropped up.'

This, had Parker but known it at the time, was only the beginning ... 'A few weeks later, Guttmann again saw me and said we must have a heat chamber for his sweating research which, if necessary, must be made by me in the workshop.' By studying the pattern of sweating – discovering which parts of the paralysed body still sweat – an accurate map can be drawn of which nerves are damaged and which are still intact. This remained one of Guttmann's most absorbing areas of scientific investigation. 'Materials were very scarce at that time, so I could not help but reply:

"From what?" This difficulty, in spite of my explanations, did not appear to trouble Dr Guttmann, because he just replied that we must find some . . . and in a very short time, we set out by bus for Oxford in search of ideas and materials. On our return, I set about the construction of the heat box and by using tea chests and any scrap wood available, I completed the job at a total cost of £6 10s. The first patients to use the heat box christened it the "torture chamber", and declared that I ought to be put inside for an unlimited period for making such a contraption . . .'

Together with the daily running of the unit, Guttmann's scientific background dictated, from the very beginning, that methodical research should also be undertaken. He had badgered Bill Parker into making him the heat box which he proceeded to install in a corner of his small office. It was here that Guttmann (not infrequently dubbed 'Sweaty' by his colleagues) continued his research into disturbance of temperature regulations with the aid of his Quinizarin dye test. Joan Scruton remembers that 'Whenever I had cause to go into his office-cum-research room and there was a sweat test in progress, I was either shielded from the sight of a naked paraplegic half covered with blue powder or was called excitedly to see the results of the research which, needless to say, I never understood. I don't know what happened to that first sweat box, but really it should have become a museum piece.'

She also recalls a time after both Guttmann and his sweat box were installed in a new and larger office, when it was used on at least one occasion for an entirely different purpose. 'I found Dr Guttmann crouched in the sweat box one day, with all the electric bulbs blazing. The central heating in the hospital had failed and it was the only warm place he could find . . .'

Ludwig Guttmann (*bottom right*) with his paternal grandparents, Rose and Joseph, his sisters and cousins, during their annual summer holiday on their farm in Silesia, about 1908.

An enthusiastic member of the Jewish fencing fraternity, Thuringia, at Breslau University. Here Guttmann shows off his duelling 'scars of honour', which he kept for the rest of his life.

With his mentor, Dr Otfrid Foerster, whose chief assistant Guttmann became in 1929, at the Wenzel Hancke Krankenhaus in Breslau.

After five years' research, back working where he wanted to be –
with patients. Ludwig Guttmann ('Poppa') at the Spinal Injuries
Unit at Stoke Mandeville Hospital.

Wounded soldiers being airlifted home. The order was given, before D-Day, that wherever possible spinal cord injured casualties were to be sent straight to Stoke Mandeville.

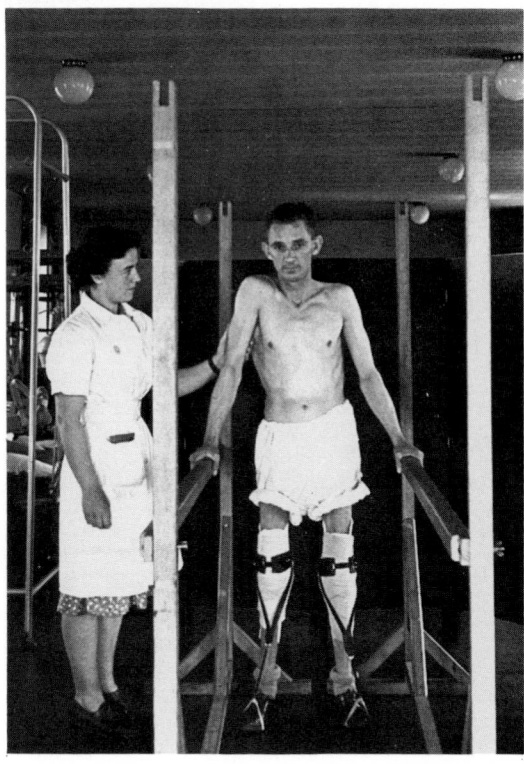

Determination plus dedication: physiotherapy at Stoke Mandeville Hospital.

The active physiotherapy department at Stoke Mandeville Hospital. To quote a paralysed former boxer: 'There's no bloody time to be ill in this bloody place!'

How the Games began. Early patients getting to grips with a wooden puck.

Guttmann was convinced that work and recreation of all kinds greatly improved the mental and physical rehabilitation of spinally injured patients. (His development of this later to include sport for the disabled was a logical outcome of these strongly held convictions – and his competitive nature.) Even before the unit opened, he had evaluated the physiotherapy department of the hospital. Aware of the needs of patients who would soon be filling his ward, he found the methods and the attitudes of the physiotherapists themselves outdated – and inadequate to his purpose. He envisaged a programme of 'purposeful, dynamic physical management' rather than the traditional, passive approach, which was mostly rather gentle massage:

'I recall the difficulties I had to put this programme into practice. While it was not difficult to get a pair of wooden parallel bars made, to get one physiotherapist to treat only paraplegia in those early days was asking too much, for no physiotherapist worth her salt could ever be expected to treat only "those chronic cripples". At my insistence, however, it was the late Mrs Joan Maynard who "nobly" stepped into the breach. She very soon realised the thrill of teaching paraplegics to re-adjust themselves to their physical deficit and still have an active life by new techniques. Her devotion, enthusiasm and success spread amongst all her younger colleagues, and in the end physiotherapists became most anxious to work entirely for paraplegics and tetraplegics, and thus became most important members of my team. One of my first physiotherapists of the unit, Miss E. Hobson, summarised admirably the fundamental change of attitude of physiotherapists which had taken place towards the problems of spinal paralysis: "From the days of dread of having to go and move some wretched immobile paraplegic's toes, hoping to avoid embarrassing questions, yet remain falsely

113

optimistic, one can now with confidence sum up the probable picture and thoroughly enjoy the years spent in helping him to become an individual – independent, mobile and reasonably fit.'

Miss Hobson, who joined the unit in the summer of 1944, remembers particularly 'all those things we tried out *for the first time* ... because there was no pattern of treatment for the physiotherapist to follow. We had to establish this for ourselves ... Now, a new dynamic approach was envisaged. But what was to be our goal? ... We did not know to what extent standing and walking would relieve spasm, or passive stretching reduce contractures. We did not know what degree of independence patients with higher or lower levels of lesion should attain.'

So the physiotherapy department at Stoke Mandeville became a pioneering venture in what was or was not possible – or helpful – in the rehabilitation of an individual patient. These new techniques of physical treatment soon attracted many physiotherapists from within Britain and abroad, both to be trained and to work, and physiotherapy schools sent pupils and teachers for day courses and lectures. Guttmann came to rely heavily on the work and the emotional commitment of his physiotherapists, and later wrote in tribute that:

'It has been our experience throughout the years that physiotherapists have become deeply interested in and fascinated by the daily problems of their patients, and with their specialist knowledge and experience they have assisted the paralysed patient to achieve a satisfactory return to the community. Moreover, by regular contact with the patient, the nursing staff as well as the physiotherapist learned of problems which might not have been revealed to other members of the team, including the doctor. They act as a vital link in the chain of communication and can pass important information to the medical officer in charge of the case and to other members of the team, which proves so helpful for the total rehabilitation of the patient.'

It was his passionate insistence on detailed research and investigation which caused one of Ludwig Guttmann's first conflicts with authority, 'the first of many', as he commented himself – always undertaken on behalf of his work or his patients. It concerned the envelopes which were allotted for keeping X-rays. These came in one size only, which meant that the larger X-rays had to be cut into two to fit and were thus rendered useless for research or publication. In Joan Scruton's words: 'Dr Guttmann did not accept that larger envelopes were not available from the Ministry of Pensions and demanded that these be supplied forthwith. Of course, he won the battle – as he usually did when fighting for the patients and the unit.' Such skirmishes with bureaucracy prompted a close associate to write of him: 'He made some enemies, but he made more friends . . .'

When Foerster died in 1941, an obituary described him as the best neurophysiologist Germany ever produced, but adding that he was more interested in establishing facts than in the fate of his patients. Professor David Whitteridge comments that 'This is not a remark anyone could ever make about Guttmann.'

He was, indeed, vitally concerned with his patients' morale, and wrote and lectured extensively on this subject. He understood that it was upon this, quite as much as upon any medical skills, that the degree of rehabilitation depended: 'Some people, when realising that they have lost control of bladder, bowel and sexual function, with no hope of a cure, are so overwhelmed that they become negative and angry . . . other patients may become completely self-centred and profoundly despondent.' Nevertheless, it was Guttmann's

experience that 'in the *majority* of paraplegics and tetraplegics, these stages of regression and denial can be overcome
by empathy on the one hand and firm dealing on the other
by medical and paramedical staff.'

Guttmann found self-written reports by patients, which
he encouraged, to be of enormous help in their overall
treatment. These reports recorded individual reactions; patients' innate attitudes towards their incapacities, their families
and society in general, freely expressed. He maintained that
all his professional life he continued to learn from his
patients. But he always believed that the single remark from
which he learnt the most – and which he never forgot or
ceased to quote – was written by the Reverend Albert Bull,
a paraplegic Army chaplain who had spent eighteen painful
months in various hospitals before arriving at Stoke Mandeville in 1944. In his report, he wrote: '*The first duty of a
paraplegic is to cheer up his visitors.*' Guttmann felt that 'This
significant remark taught me and my staff how to educate
the public to abandon its attitude of pity and replace it by
positive and practical help in returning their paralysed fellow
men and women to society.'

Those staff and patients who remember early weeks in
Ward X speak of it as 'cheerful' and 'purposeful': 'Everything bustled with activity, wheelchairs rolled from bed to
bed and limbs were being pulled this way and that by the
physios.' Guttmann's most vivid memory, recorded by him
twenty-one years later, was of 'those young heroes who came
in from the battlefronts with terrible wounds and all the
horrible complications of mismanagement one could
imagine, and of the extremely limited facilities which existed
for their treatment.' But despite these limitations – the shortages, the lack of space, the war-time 'making-do' – the unit
was moving in the direction Guttmann intended. By the end
of that year, 1944, a successful experiment was carried out

with a local firm in Aylesbury to employ six paralysed and rehabilitated soldiers who were still being treated. Noted by the Ministry of Labour, this resulted in Industrial Rehabilitation Centres being set up in different parts of the country.

As the late Dora Bell, Superintendent Physiotherapist, believed, 'the bearer of hope for paraplegics', in the person of Ludwig Guttmann, was established. By August, there were almost fifty patients at the unit. Guttmann's dynamic, authoritarian leadership, his devotion to his work, his attention to detail, paid dividends: from the first day, he had begun to weld his nucleus of a staff into a team. Perhaps they didn't quite know why at that time – but they believed in him. Short, stocky, bespectacled, he moved quickly, as though perpetually in a hurry. He worked tirelessly. To Joan Scruton, caught up in his vision from the first, the man – and his work – seemed 'so alive'. To one bewildered early patient he was 'all over the place, like a tornado'. Another said: 'He was the most *determined* man I have ever met.'

In any event, he was making his mark and making it quickly. Brigadier General Riddoch's unexpected appointment was turning out well. Ludwig Guttmann's methods and his organisation of the new Spinal Injuries Unit at Stoke Mandeville were noticed. And in May 1944, just three months after the first patient had been admitted, Riddoch gave orders that wherever possible all spinal injuries from the planned D-Day landings were to be sent to Stoke Mandeville.

Life with 'Poppa'

———◆◆———

'WE CALLED SIR LUDWIG "POPPA" for almost as long as I can remember,' Joan Scruton said, thinking back across the span of forty years. 'He really was the father of the centre. We all had so much faith in him ... everyone went to him when they were in trouble. Later, when the Spinal Injuries Centre at Stoke Mandeville became an international byword, and through the development of the Games for the Paralysed, he became a father of the paraplegic movement world-wide ...'

Those who still remember the unit in the late 1940s – patients and staff – speak of it with a mixture of awe and affection. It was, they agree, a very special place to be. Guttmann always believed that timing, or 'fate' as he preferred to call it, played an unusually large part in the dramatic twists and turns of his life. He would point out the pure chance which led him to take up neurology in the first place; his recall by Foerster from his promising position in Friedrichsberg to become his assistant; his family's bitter flight from their home in Nazi Germany; the two papers he wrote in Oxford which so impressed Brigadier General Riddoch that he offered him the appointment at Stoke Mandeville.

Exactly sixteen months after the first patient was admitted to the unit, the war, in Europe, at least, was over. Nationally, it was a time of hardship but also of hope, as the country attempted to rebuild and plan for a future which had often seemed bleak and uncertain. 'Fate' – or timing – was on Ludwig Guttmann's side again. For his pioneering work in paraplegia at Stoke Mandeville Hospital seemed to echo this national sense of purpose. From the beginning, he struck a note of optimism where there had been none. He set out to prove that by strict application of the methods he had evolved both through his experience and his research – and frequently despite the scepticism of his colleagues – these young men and women, severely injured in the service of their country, could be rehabilitated to lead useful lives within the community. He was determined that unlike similarly wounded ex-servicemen of the First World War, whose plight had so affected both Guttmann in Germany and Riddoch working as a doctor behind British lines, these youngsters, like their country, had a future. At that time, to the medical profession and to the man in the street, this was an extraordinary concept. But with unerring belief in the medical sense and moral justification of his ambitions, from 1 February 1944 Guttmann set out to do a job which nobody else wanted or thought feasible.

During those first crucial months and years of the unit, it seemed that something of the positive war-time mentality did prevail among his staff: the sense of pitching in and pulling together for a common goal. And Guttmann's zeal for his work was catching. He inspired.

Dr Jack Walsh came to Stoke Mandeville on 1 January 1947 as a junior medical officer. 'It was an exceptionally hard winter with two feet of snow around the hospital for months. One of my most vivid memories is of standing with Dr Guttmann in the bitter cold – indoors but still wrapped in overcoats – waiting to receive approximately fifteen new patients from a spinal unit which had just been closed.' By that time, there were some sixty to ninety beds in the Spinal

Injuries Unit, which had grown rapidly since the D-Day landings, spreading along the south side of the hospital.'

Guttmann saw every patient on the unit at least once a week. He conducted his ward rounds in the tradition of the teaching hospitals, as he had been trained in Germany, accompanied by assistant doctors, the sister, physiotherapist, occupational therapist – 'the whole retinue', as Dr Walsh put it. These were not always comfortable occasions. Guttmann could be brutally outspoken; at times, both patients and staff felt humiliated by such public scrutiny. But if anyone dared to remonstrate, Guttmann always insisted that he was not nearly as hard on *his* staff as Otfrid Foerster had been on him.

More than anything else, looking back to those days, Dr Walsh recalls Guttmann's brilliance as a teacher. 'He had a superb knowledge of neurophysiology which he was able to get across through his own passionate interest in the subject – and the force of his personality.' He conducted teaching ward rounds about once a week, after work, from 4.30 to 6.30 p.m. Individual cases were presented and commented upon by Guttmann and the medical staff. 'Guttmann pressured his staff relentlessly,' Dr Walsh said. 'If a junior member didn't know an answer or didn't speak up clearly enough, he was ticked off, publicly, in no uncertain terms. But the quality of Dr Guttmann's teaching at these sessions was remarkable. Although they might not want to admit it, quite a few of his most senior colleagues, from all over the country, attended from time to time.' When the unit was established and gaining a reputation, Guttmann's brilliant teaching and successful treatment of paraplegia certainly did attract colleagues and students, not just from Britain but throughout the world to Stoke Mandeville.

Dr Walsh: 'At the drop of a hat he would take on anyone, up to and including the Permanent Undersecretary of the

Ministry of Pensions, as it was in those days, if he felt it was in the interest of his patients and the unit ... he always had one or two good rows brewing ... Whatever he did – on the wards, his research, his publications – he always worked hard.'

Dr Walsh remembers that about once a month Guttmann would sweep all the senior staff off to what was then the Bull's Head, the oldest pub in Aylesbury. There, just as over the fine wines he had shared in Breslau with Foerster many years before, tensions built up over long working hours eased. In a relaxed atmosphere, away from the hospital, shop talk, stories and reminiscences were exchanged with the drinks. Guttmann found these sessions extremely valuable in getting to know, and assessing, his staff. In fact parties, on the wards or among staff members, became regular features at the Spinal Injuries Unit. The anniversary of its founding, 1 February, was celebrated every year – and is to this day.

Another early recruit to the unit was Sister E. McElhinney, who exchanged the 8th Army and Field Marshal Montgomery for Stoke Mandeville and Ludwig Guttmann. However, as she admits, her initial reactions to her new position were not favourable:

'With my Army medals safely tucked away, I said goodbye to my Army life and once more became a civilian. To my horror, I was detailed by the matron to do holiday relief on the spinal unit! What a let down! I, with all my wonderful and valuable 8th Army experience to be wasted, as I then thought, on chronic nursing! However, having been endowed with a fair amount of curiosity and a larger amount of 8th Army determination, I decided to give it a trial. But it was with a very hypercritical attitude that I took up my duties.

'Five days passed before I was to meet the doctor in charge of the unit, who had been described by my colleagues as a slightly terrifying person. I did not find him terrifying – not after Monty! – but I did think he had the oddest ideas.

'Gradually, this work began to interest me, for there was a purpose and an enthusiasm about this doctor which was very infectious. As I toured the unit in my relief capacity, it soon became quite obvious to me that the spinal unit was a very happy place in which to work, and that the morale of the patients and staff was very high. But even more surprising was my own fast-changing attitude to this work, which I was now beginning to find most satisfying and rewarding. My previous experience of paraplegics had been of those I had seen in the different Army hospitals, screened off at the end of the wards and slowly dying of sepsis and emaciation from the two complications hitherto considered as inevitable – pressure sores and kidney deficiency. I was now learning that it was quite wrong to have a defeatist attitude towards paraplegics and that here was a unit which was really doing something for them.

'In February 1948, I took over Ward X, and then the spinal bug really got me and I became its slave. No sister could wish for a more satisfying job. Never a dull moment! Dr Guttmann kept us all on our toes with new treatments and more research. General Montgomery's famous phrase has never applied more aptly: "The difficult we do at once, the impossible takes a little longer."'

Sister McElhinney's radically changed attitudes towards nursing the spinally injured – her conversion to Guttmann's methods and philosophy – were shared by several key paramedical workers assigned to the unit at the same time. The late Dora Bell remembered that 'In the autumn of 1943 rumour reached the physiotherapy department that a whole ward was to be set aside for these apparently dead-end patients. We were in fact to have a paraplegic unit! It was rumoured, too, that a doctor would be coming whose sole duty would be to treat these patients. Surely any doctor who intended to devote his whole time to the treatment of paraplegics (tetraplegics were not envisaged at that time) must have some ideas other than the making of string bags and other such useless occupations. Dr Guttmann made his first appearance in the physiotherapy department, and although on that day I never for one moment envisaged the magnitude of his work, it is always a satisfaction to me to remember that I was one of the very first to welcome his arrival. . . .

'Immediately he asked for a pair of parallel bars and a physiotherapist to treat his patients. He rejected massage for his patients; this would be replaced by activity. Although a somewhat odd request, we thought it would not be difficult to find parallel bars, but the kind of bars Dr Guttmann had in mind were very different from the heavy and cumbersome ones used in a gymnasium, and we waited in vain for what he wanted. One day a medical orderly had the bright idea to convert two balkam bars for our purpose, and so came the portable parallel bars now commonly used in the rehabilitation of paraplegics.

'One of the very first patients in the unit was a young Cockney soldier with a very low lesion at the base of the spinal cord causing partial paralysis of the legs and bladder and bowels. He was so stiff that he could have been lifted up by his toes in one piece. It fell to the lot of Mrs Maynard to treat this patient, and because he had sensation, the pain on passive movement was excruciating. These two battled on until at last his joints began to loosen up, and one day, to the utter amazement of everyone, Guttmann announced that he should stand. Physiotherapists gathered round with

Guttmann at the helm, while this pioneer patient was heaved to his feet. . . .'

Elvira Hobson had joined the staff in the summer of 1944. Her most vivid recollections are of 'Patients wearing hospital blues perhaps; or tidal drainage equipment set up by nearly every bedside; the sweat box – Dr Guttmann's pet research; or "push-pulls" wheeling round the countryside; above all, the camaraderie of war-time days.'

She stresses the experimental nature of the physiotherapy which was practised in the unit – 'things we tried out for the *first time* but with a good deal of anxiety'. She adds that 'Because of the co-operation of those first paraplegic patients and their tremendous willingness to try out new ideas, along with their ingenuity in suggesting more, and their dogged perseverance in battling, often against seemingly overwhelming odds, a programme eventually emerged and a pattern was built up. A new way of life was forged little by little for all those who were to follow.'

Inevitably, strong and enduring bonds grew between staff and patients and between the patients themselves. Guttmann encouraged healthy competitiveness and when progress was made, he wanted it to be seen. For example, Professor Whitteridge remembers that 'When a patient took his first steps, often in light walking callipers to fix the knees, he did so not in the physiotherapy department but in the middle of the ward, so that other patients could see that there was hope for them too.'

For it was Ludwig Guttmann's particular talent to be able to cajole or bully patients, in whatever ratio he felt necessary, into making the most of their remaining physical capacities. This was his undoubted gift. (It was not false modesty which made an eminent colleague say of him: 'He – Guttmann – could get patients to perform in a way I could not.') A few

resented his authoritarian manner; most came, sometimes
grudgingly, to love and revere him. He was a character; he
had a way with him. His strong German accent provoked
surprise and, sometimes, amusement. His short stature gave
patients either prone or in wheelchairs the impression, at
least, that they could pat him on the head; or so one of
them remembered, smiling, many years after. Dr Walsh is
emphatic that during the first years, when the unit was
beginning to make an impact in the field of paraplegia, 'The
admiration of both patients and staff for Dr Guttmann just
grew and grew.' Many of these patients came from hospitals
where they had received practically no treatment, as was
standard at that time, and were usually in appalling physical
condition. The *hope* that the Spinal Injuries Unit engendered
was nothing short of lifegiving. Eloquent testimony of this
is given by a patient who was brought to the unit by
Guttmann soon after the end of the war – in despair:

When I lay wounded in a military hospital in Brussels
(the date was 17 January 1945) I saw and heard General
Montgomery, as he was then, standing in the middle
of the ward and saying, 'Well, chaps, you have done a
good job, and you are going back to be treated by the
finest doctors and nurses in the world.'

I was to realise this the day I entered Stoke Mandeville ...

As a soldier in the Royal Army Medical Corps, I,
more than most, realised what it meant to suffer so
severe a wound as the severing of my spinal cord.
This was confirmed for me at an Emergency Medical
Services Hospital by the ward doctor, who told me I
would never walk again, and even though I knew it,
my spirit reached the bottom of despair, that I, who had
been so active and enjoyed life so much, was doomed to

a wheelchair ... It was a blow that I did not think I could take.

It was some months later, as I lay in bed indulging in self-pity and thinking of the things I could have done in life, that I noticed a little man walking from bed to bed with the ward sister, till finally he arrived at mine, and greeted me with a cheery 'Good morning', to which I replied 'Is it?' He then asked the sister how my temperature was over a period and she answered, 'Normal.' I promptly countered this with 'How can anyone be normal with no feeling in half of one's body?' He then turned to me and said, 'I am Dr Guttmann, and I have just opened a spinal unit at Stoke Mandeville, near Aylesbury, and I should like you to come as a patient. If you come I will have you out of bed and working in two or three weeks.' This statement, made so confidently to me, was one that seemed ridiculous at the time and I answered 'What me? In my state of health?'

It is now many years since that day, and that was a remark I have never forgotten and a remark Dr Guttmann never forgot. Because I was admitted to Stoke Mandeville and three weeks later to the day I was dressing myself and working in the cobblers' shop in the hospital.

Never losing sight of his true objective – to return the majority of his patients to the community as self-sufficient citizens – Guttmann insisted on *work* as a part of every patient's therapy. Pre-vocational workshops were set up in the hospital where patients could do woodwork, instrument-making and clock- and watch-repairing. All patients were forcefully encouraged to fulfil their potential despite traumatic injury. One young officer, admitted to the unit in June

1944, passed his first law examination in ten months while still at Stoke Mandeville. Professor Whitteridge writes of a severely injured ex-jockey who 'at first wished to refuse treatment and die, but then became interested in sport again and re-acquired a will to live. He took correspondence courses in elementary arithmetic and training in accountancy in the administrator's office, was give free articles by a chartered accountant and passed his final examination in accountancy.'

Gradually, under 'Poppa's' demanding regime, a close-knit, almost family atmosphere evolved at the unit. Work was the order of the day for patients and staff alike. Many of the staff lived at the hospital; Guttmann commuted to and from Oxford at weekends as best he could, until the family moved to High Wycombe in 1951.

'Perhaps *secretary* is rather a loose term for the Jack-of-all-trades that I really was in those early days,' Joan Scruton said. 'Then, my duties were also those of welfare officer and instructor in commerce, there being no one else available for these functions at that time. I don't know that the hours I spent trying to teach some of the fellows shorthand and typing had any actual educational value, but they were certainly interesting!

'With no television and no such things as manual control cars or motor tricycles for paraplegics, we had to make our own amusements. This we did in many varied ways, including the "choir on wheels" and drama society. There were also the concerts, sometimes held in the wards themselves as well as in the gymnasium. A glint came into Dr Guttmann's eye when he recalled the concert given by the Windmill Girls in the canteen! Often, we would hold whist drives in the wards which, with more than half the players in bed, were great fun if somewhat unorthodox. Sometimes we would push patients up to the "local", where as often as not the evening would develop into a grand "sing-song", finishing inevitably with the landlady singing "We'll gather Lilacs" with great fervour and power.'

Cars were few in those post-war years and petrol scarce; there was no television; amusements were homely: whist, sing-songs, belaboured visits to the local pubs in outmoded 'push–pulls' – the first light, folding wheelchairs became available only in about 1949. One remembered highlight of this in-house entertainment was a revue called *Life With Poppa*, written and performed by patients of both sexes. All the performers were immaculately attired in full make-up and evening dress and the performance definitely had professional polish, as well as its share of backstage near-disasters. The script drew heavily on Guttmann's idiosyncratic leadership and inspired a good deal of mirth among insiders. 'Did you see Poppa roar when we got to that bit about him in the Physio?' one satisfied member of the cast was heard to enquire of another.

As with any successful venture, the loyalty and dedication of those who worked at the unit, in whatever capacity, was crucial. These stalwarts included Bill Parker, who developed the workshops; Miss Medford, the first matron; D.M. French, who started as controller of the stores' office, later becoming welfare officer; clinical photographer Jimmy Riddle, recruited by Guttmann even before his six weeks' demob leave was up; and Charlie Atkinson, the physiotherapist who found himself a pioneer in the movement of sport for the disabled.

As early as 1944, Guttmann's restless search for ways to prod his apathetic patients back into meaningful life had led him to investigate the possibilities of sport. Simple ball games were followed by archery, netball and table-tennis – the beginning of the concept of sport for the disabled. With mandatory work already established and now sport, plus the non-stop treatment by the physiotherapists, constantly trying out new exercises, Stoke Mandeville's Spinal Injuries Unit became known, somewhat surprisingly, for its ceaseless activity. One story which became legendary was of a paralysed former boxer on the ward who was heard to complain one day that 'There's no bloody time to be ill in this bloody place ...'

In 1947 Guttmann founded a magazine, *The Cord*, which he intended to be written and edited *for* and *by* paraplegics, hoping that it would establish a link between patients who had been at the unit, and serve as a platform for his views on the treatment and rehabilitation of spinal cord injury victims. The project, like the unit, flourished. The editor for many years was Dudley Sutton. More than most, he had reason to be grateful to *The Cord*. A chance reading of one of the early editions had led him to Stoke Mandeville and to Ludwig Guttmann after many years of spinal cord disease which had become increasingly intractable. After treatment at the unit he obtained a post in the administrative office of a London teaching hospital, a job he was well qualified for but which was clinched for him, he wrote, 'by the good offices of Dr Guttmann'. While working full-time, he edited *The Cord* for many years and was responsible for the twenty-first anniversary issue, a remarkable record of the emergence of a new direction in modern medicine.

Two early contributors were David Chard and Reg Townsend. Chard had been wounded on active service in Italy, Townsend in France shortly after D-Day. In the summer of 1945, they found themselves in the same ward at Stoke Mandeville as patients of Ludwig Guttmann; both ebullient personalities, they got to know each other well. Twenty-one years later they looked back and remembered, vividly recalling that time when the end of the war at last appeared to be in sight; and when, in most places other than Stoke Mandeville, paraplegics were still considered hopeless cripples.

23 June 1944

I had been in the Ranville-Breville area for seventeen days, and had suffered no more than discomfort from shaving in cold water – apart from being scared to death – and when Nemesis or whomsoever it was tapped me on the shoulder, it was an anti-climax. On Montgomery's behalf I had a half-a-dozen men snugly hidden between a high bank and two six-foot walls of earth-filled ammo-boxes, furiously – and I mean furiously – digging a new latrine.

We had reached a depth of about six feet when the Germans began swamping the area with mortar-bombs. After giving the matter serious thought, it took me two seconds to tell the blokes to get in the trench – and I set them a good example.

The bomb hit a branch just above us and showered down. One of the blokes caught a fragment in the head and I felt a blow on the back of my neck. I had an immediate sensation of floating in the air – most peculiar – but when I tried to move and found that I couldn't, I knew that I had caught it in the spine.

Within five minutes I was in the dressing-station and it was not long after that that an ambulance was taking me to the base hospital. I did not at any time lose track of anything until they put me out in the theatre to insert a suprapubic catheter, a means of draining the urine from my now unco-operative bladder.

A Dakota flew me to Swindon and from there a horrible bouncy utility-truck took me to St Hughes at Oxford. After about three weeks I was sent to a place called Stoke Mandeville where, I was told, I would be under expert care.

My first experience of this haven of rest was singularly painful. For the flight from Normandy, the medics there had encased my head and shoulders in a plaster cast which a certain benevolent looking gentleman with a heavy accent informed me, must come off. An angelic blonde nurse promptly belied her looks by hacking at me with an enormous pair of garden shears which had to be forced up between my head and the plaster in order to cut my hair, which was firmly embedded in said plaster. Don't let anybody tell you that the Americans invented the crew-cut.

I had to be fed, washed, shaved, the lot – which I thought was fair enough. But not on your life. The benevolent gentleman, one Dr Guttmann, startled me more than somewhat by telling me not to be lazy, to help myself. It was not until some years later that I realised what a devilish technique the good doctor employed. He made me so bloody mad that I used extra energy just to relieve my feelings.

Partitioned off at the end of Ward 1 was a sinister ante-room where, at the hands of a long succession of different doctors, me and my ilk were subjected to the "sweat box", a table that acted like a drawbridge with, of course, a victim strapped upon it, and many weird and wonderful devices too complex to enumerate.

From out of all this emerged a whole fund of knowledge and facts – and some very limp paraplegics.

Gradually a pattern of life took shape which was resisted every foot of the way by us who would ultimately benefit from it. Each innovation was greeted with shocked incredulity. Clock-making, engineering and carpentry, on top of the usual occupational therapy.

131

The latter I am glad to say I was able to dodge, in spite of the valiant efforts of the hard-working staff.

Then came the male-voice choir which, in spite of our scepticism, gave us and, I think, others, some pleasure. In the same vein we embarked upon a production of *Libel*. It started just as a play reading, but as we progressed our enthusiasm grew and before long we were talking about putting it on. We had every encouragement from Dr Guttmann. We finished up by putting on a public performance at the Aylesbury Theatre.

It was just after *Libel* that I had to have a bladder-resection which brought my blood count down to thirty, and visits from Dr Walsh at unearthly hours of the morning, for which I was grateful.

In the early days Dr Guttmann had told me that I would get on my feet some time and do some work. I was much too polite to say the first words that came into my head and in any case, I don't think that Poppa would have at that time understood that sort of English.

But with the aid of plasters to brace my legs, and later, calipers, I did, with much sweat and passing-out, get on my feet and move up and down the length of parallel bars.

By the morning of Tuesday, 18 January 1949, I was firmly ensconced as a senior member of the Stoke Old Boys Club (headquarters – The Bell, Stoke Mandeville) when on his weekly round Dr Guttmann told me without a blink that I would be going to Chaseley – a residence on the seafront at Eastbourne – in two days' time!

Outrage could hardly describe my feelings – I was betrayed. Ward 2 was my home and had been for four and a half years – he couldn't shift me. But he did. My faith in human nature was shattered.

The ambulance that deposited me at Chaseley took David Chard back to Stoke for major surgery, and with him went the only man I would have really known at my new home. Poppa's ears should have been burning.

Without really trying, I had been called the laziest man at Stoke, so I could never understand how it was that on 7 March I was interviewed at Chaseley by an official of the Dental Estimates Board with a view to my employment at that establishment, and I started work on 14 March 1949.

Despite occasional setbacks, after his release from the unit, Reg Townsend held a full-time job for many years. He married and had a son. Ending his piece in *The Cord* he wrote:

> I would not recommend paraplegia to anybody as a career, but if it falls your way there is only one place to go, and there you will find the finest team in the world, led, as from the beginning, by one man.

*　　*　　*

'I walked and ran, I jumped and swam, I loved – serving in the Army in Italy I was, as the Services termed it, A.1.'

That is how David Chard remembered the way he was, a young man serving with the Allied Forces in Italy:

> In April 1944, in Italy, I was introduced to paraplegia, although I did not know it at the time. Shrapnel shattered my spine and the nerves therein, and I had stood on my unsupported legs for the last time.

133

Having regained enough strength to take notice of life, I found myself in a hospital in Rimini. I was told that I had been operated upon, and protruding from my stomach was a tube which was apparently a catheter – a means of draining urine. This tube and I were going to be friends for years.

As yet, I was undaunted. Not being able to move my legs held no real significance for me, as doctors, nurses and orderlies kept telling me it was 'early days yet', and I had no reason to disbelieve them. I was moved from hospital to hospital, and when in August 1944 I was eventually shipped home to England my hopes rose, for surely now it would not be long before I should be well again. It was perhaps better that I did not know the truth.

Unknown to me, some of the side-effects of a paralysed body were beginning to manifest themselves. Pressure sores were developing and worse still, stones were forming in my kidney.

Day after day I was expected to die, and vomiting and complete despair were my constant companions. Eventually, a brother who lived in London brought news of a spinal unit at Stoke Mandeville and insisted that I be transferred there, and on 21 June 1945, I found myself at 'Stoke'.

I entered Ward 2 on a stretcher, to find everything bustling with activity, wheelchairs rolling from bed to bed and limbs being pulled this way and that. Within a few minutes I had been examined by a cheerful young doctor called Dr Jonason, who was shortly afterwards joined by a short, bespectacled man who proved to be Dr Guttmann and who I gathered was the 'Boss'.

From that moment, my treatment was started in real earnest. Throughout the night I was turned like a turkey on a spit every two hours; had it been practicable, we would even have been stood on our heads! It seems we were not meant to sleep at Stoke Mandeville. I had an operation to remove the stones from my right kidney and another one later on to remove shrapnel from my spine. Slowly, my sores began to heal and I began to regain strength, and the world looked rosy once more. The physiotherapist attending me slowly but surely began to loosen my utterly contracted legs and body, although there were times when I thought her intentions were to snap my legs off at the knees.

During all this time, the figure of Dr Guttmann loomed everywhere; early morning, late at night, he was around – it appeared he did not need food or sleep!

October 1945 – nineteen months after being wounded – was the turning point in my recuperation, when I was allowed to get out of bed. As soon as I was lifted into a wheelchair the room spun around and I was glad to get straight back into bed, never wanting to leave it again! However, the process was repeated daily, until I was able to be chairborne for hours.

Orders from the 'Boss' continued to pour out: 'He must dress, he must do some work, he must do some walking.' My day seemed to be occupied with everything except rest – me, who was paralysed!!

My rehabilitation did not take five minutes; month after month passed by, broken by 'flare ups' which put me back to bed for weeks. For me, it was still a transitional period, from self-consciousness to self-confidence. Alone, I would have failed, but prompted by Dr Guttmann and his staff the miracle worked. In 1947, Dr Walsh had joined the unit, also dedicated to the task of helping paraplegics, and the combination of Dr Guttmann, the founder, and Dr Walsh had begun.

1948 came and with it my departure from Stoke Mandeville but not, I am glad to say from the care of Stoke Mandeville, as I was sent to Chaseley at Eastbourne, where Dr Guttmann was the consultant. Full employment for his patients was ever his aim, and sure enough work came my way in a government office, which I continued for fifteen years or so.'

Today, David Chard is retired, lives with his wife in Sussex – and stays in touch with 'Stoke'.

*   *   *

By the time Susan Masham arrived at Stoke Mandeville – fourteen years after Reg Townsend and David Chard – it was firmly established as one of the leading spinal units in the world. Guttmann, whose reputation had grown along with it and with the development of the Games for the Paralysed, was still Director. Lady Masham, who was made a life peer in 1970, wrote her history for the anniversary issue of *The Cord*. And although her life and background were very different from those of the first ex-service men and women patients, her memories of 'Stoke' show that she was similarly imbued with 'Poppa's' resilience, discipline – and hope:

In spring 1958 I received a spinal injury whilst riding in a point-to-point race. Immediately after the accident I was taken to a hospital in Swindon with my unofficial fiance accompanying me in the ambulance. After a night of haemorrhage and blood transfusions, the following day I was transferred to Stoke Mandeville.

Before long I realised the importance of spinal patients being in a specialised unit. There are always severely disabled patients who set standards for the less disabled. To be in a general hospital where paraplegic patients are not understood should be avoided at all costs.

I passed through a stage of acute agony, having broken ribs and severe bruising. I used to get cramp in my shoulder and, not daring to move, used to lie moaning until my next 'turn'. At this stage I learnt the real qualities of a good nurse. There was one at the time in our ward who possessed all the qualities, but her biggest asset was her sense of humour. She is a nun and is now out in Africa, where I am sure this comes in useful.

I found there were certain visitors who did me so much good I felt I had had a tonic. One of these was a mad racing friend who tried to feed me with my supper of tinned tomatoes, which he promptly spilled inside my bed and who, on accidentally knocking the winchester hanging under my bed, said, 'I suppose it must be milking time.' But there were others – such as close relatives – who were really hard going!

After a short time a paraplegic who had been watching my race on television and had seen the fall came to visit me, and told me that after he had heard I had gone to Stoke he knew I was a paraplegic for life. He explained what this entailed and I accepted it without blinking an eyelid; but about six weeks later when one of the doctors told me, I rebelled and said I *would* ride my horse – it just depends how one is told.

The relationship between physiotherapist and patient is most important and I had a wonderful one – we became, and still are, firm friends.

My most difficult experience of all was to keep to hospital regulations and at the same time to keep an impatient fiance pacified – I knew my future depended on both these things. I accomplished neither well, but just managed to scrape through! Never will I forget the time when, returning to Stoke after dinner, I was agitating to be back at 9.30p.m. While turning the car round we slipped into a ditch. Nothing David could do could budge the car – he had to walk about two miles to a garage and telephone the hospital for transport. By the time I arrived back it was midnight. I thought I would be leaving next day! Another unforgettable incident was when a certain well-known Scottish night sister found David in the ward a few moments after he should have left: she chased him down to the end of the ward where someone let him out of the day room door. David, with sister in hot pursuit, disappeared into the night with the patients still shouting the odds.

A spinal unit could be a depressing place, but not Stoke, which was a place of hope and progress – full of interesting people and activities.

We had a wonderful Hallowe'en Party in the ward, organised by a friend and myself. When we decided to have the party we soon learnt how helpful people could be. Outside visitors gave help and suggestions; the people who could came in fancy dress. Among them were two stunning Sisters, who turned out to be two of the cervical boys!

When the time came for me to leave I felt the wrench of saying goodbye to many friends, and going into the world again.

Wheelchair Games

———◆◆◆———

THE HOT SUMMER SUNDAY OF 22 JULY 1984 was a momentous day for the British Paraplegic Sports Society and, indeed, in the history of sport for the disabled. The seventh World Wheelchair Games opened at the Ludwig Guttmann Sports Centre for the Disabled at Stoke Mandeville. His Royal Highness the Prince of Wales, Patron of the British Para-plegic Sports Society, performed the opening ceremony in the grounds of the centre. Facing the smartly assembled line-up of one thousand and eighty athletes and their escorts, who represented forty-two different countries, Prince Charles addressed them. They made him 'humble' he said.

Hundreds of spectators stood in the brilliant mid-morning sunlight as the National Anthem was played, followed by the Anthem of the International Stoke Mandeville Games, during which the Games flag was raised. A disabled athlete – Terry Willett of the United Kingdom, the host country – wheeled on to the six-lane track bearing the torch and sped past the dais to ignite the bowl containing the Olympic flame. Two other wheelchair athletes, also from Great Britain, took the Olympic oath, one on behalf of all the competitors, the other on behalf of all the judges and officials. Pigeons were released and wheeled overhead. The Prince of Wales stepped down from the dais and moved from team to team up and down the ranks of the competitors. The Paralympics were on.

However, as members of the British Paraplegic Sports Society and their many helpers were fully aware, the fact that they were taking place at all was a triumph. The United States was the Olympic country in 1984 and it was anticipated that the Paralympic Games would be held there also. An appropriate site was located, and approved, at the University of Illinois in Campaigne. Then in April, to the dismay of everyone involved and particularly the competitors, it was announced that funds necessary to hold the Games could not, after all, be raised in the United States. Joan Scruton, as Secretary General of the International Stoke Mandeville Games Federation, remembers a hastily convened meeting at the sports centre which was also attended by representatives of foreign member nations. That day the decision was taken to mount the seventh Paralympics at Stoke Mandeville. The Games would not be cancelled; the hundreds of athletes who had trained hard towards this goal would not be disappointed; the Olympic flame would be lit for them as for the able-bodied.

Ludwig Guttmann, who was still Chairman of the Executive and Director of the Sports Centre of the BPSS at his death in 1980, would have applauded this decision. He always relished a challenge; to him, no effort was too great to be made on behalf of sport for the paralysed. But the immediate problems which the committee faced were truly formidable – the normal four years of detailed planning must somehow be crammed into less than four months. The most immediate hurdles – enlarged accommodation for the competing teams and the inevitable fund-raising – were those which Ludwig Guttmann had faced, and surmounted, for more than thirty years.

Appropriately, those seventh World Wheelchair Games – but the first in the 'World' category to be held in Britain in the Games twenty-four years of existence – were dedicated to his memory and to his vow: 'We will build a sports stadium and an Olympic village so that the disabled athletes of the world will always have their own Olympic facilities here at Stoke Mandeville when other doors are closed to them.'

At the opening, Guttmann's presence – the vitality, the twinkle in the eyes behind the glasses, the gutteral accent – were missed by many; by athletes who would be competing in the events during the next two weeks, by officials, and by the many spectators who crowded round to watch the ceremonies. So much of his heart and mind had gone into every aspect of these games. His daughter, Eva, who was there, was reminded of a basketball match during the International Stoke Mandeville Games some years before: 'One of the competitors fell out of his chair. Typically, quick as a flash as usual, Poppa was the first one there to push him back.'

But that opening was a triumphant occasion, and 'Poppa' always loved success. The presence of the Royal Patron, Prince Charles – on unusually short notice – lent pomp and colour. The teams, led by twenty-seven athletes from Austria, complete with Tyrolean hats, began the slow wheel-past. The band played and the flags of the competing countries flew gaily. Over the loudspeakers came Esther Rantzen's buoyant commentary. The crowd, stirred by the emotive sight of these hundreds of wheelchair athletes gliding past, clapped enthusiastically and gave a special hand to the teams from the two countries entering for the first time – Papua New Guinea and Zimbabwe. Weeks later, the most successful of these competitors would be taking part in demonstration events at the Olympic Games in Los Angeles.

The idea of competitive sport for the disabled goes back forty years before that spectacular Paralympic opening wheelpast. It arose from quite a mundane incident which occurred just a few hundred yards from where the sports centre now stands. In the autumn of 1944, Ludwig Guttmann came upon a group of his patients frantically propelling their wheelchairs on the flat surface outside the unit, attempting to hit a wooden puck with upended walking sticks. Immediately, his interest was caught. For some time he had been seriously concerned with finding ways to alleviate the boredom and depression of young disabled war veterans. He had already succesfully instigated punchball exercises, darts, skittles and snooker. Now, he suddenly saw broader possibilities – genuine *wheelchair sports*.

Without wasting a moment, Guttmann himself got straight into a wheelchair: 'I tried to move about and, using the curved handle of a walking stick hit the ball and chased after it. Simultaneously, I tried to prevent my opponent in another wheelchair – the physical instructor of the hospital – from counteracting my movements.' However clumsy these initial performances, Guttmann later wrote in his *Textbook for the Disabled* that 'they taught me two valuable lessons. The first, that wheelchair polo, as I had already termed it in my mind, was possible as a competitive team sport for paraplegics. And secondly, judging from my own and my opponent's difficulty in manoeuvring the chair and keeping our legs still, a sport was about to be created in which the paraplegic was clearly less handicapped than the able-bodied.'

A Belgian doctor, Professor A. Tricot, who worked closely with Guttmann for over thirty years, once said of him that 'When Guttmann was on to an idea, nothing could stop him.' So it was with sport ...

On Guttmann's staff in 1944 was Quartermaster Sergeant Instructor Thomas Hill, known to everyone as 'Q'. He had been temporarily assigned to the hospital by the Army and it was his job to improve the physical condition of patients who could still walk, so that they could be returned to their Army units. Dora Bell recalled: 'Dr Guttmann soon had "Q" in his spinal wards throwing and catching balls with the bed patients, to the utter amazement of the sister in charge. This was very revolutionary indeed . . . Our thoughts were now turned to remedial sport. Patients in big brown wheelchairs began to play wheelchair polo against a team of physiotherapists, likewise in brown wheelchairs. Then, one afternoon, Dr Guttmann arrived in the physiotherapy department with a bow and arrow, and commanded that we were going to teach the patients archery!'

After some hazardous months of trial, wheelchair polo was abandoned. As Joan Scruton described it: 'Polo, using wheelchairs as "mounts", shortened walking sticks and a little wooden disc proved a stimulating if somewhat rough sport, particularly for the local footballers or physiotherapy staff against whom our players pitted their skills. Surveying the carnage after a more than usually boisterous match, Dr Guttmann decided that polo must give way to basketball.'

Over the years, basketball has become one of the most popular sports for the disabled athlete. Played at a high standard, it is fast, skilful and thrilling to watch. The international basketball final in the 1984 Paralympics at Stoke Mandeville between France and Holland was breathtaking and the hard-fought match generated huge excitement among the spectators jamming the hot and noisy stadium.

But in 1944, as the end of the war was in sight, the idea of disabled people playing serious competitive sport still seemed ridiculous. In fact, Guttmann's experimental manoeuvrings in a wheelchair had been, as he knew, soundly based in medical thinking. Many years later, in his definitive *Textbook*, he wrote:

143

'At all times, members of the medical profession concerned with the management of deformities and other forms of physical disability, have included exercise in their treatment ...' He cited the ancient medical author Galen and, in medieval times, his follower Maimonides, who offered this eminently sensible advice: 'Anyone who lives a sedentary life and does not exercise, even if he eats good food and takes care of himself according to proper medical principles – all his days will be painful ones and his strength shall wane.' Remedial gymnastics for the treatment of physical disabilities, under medical supervision, had been widely accepted throughout Europe during the nineteenth century.

Convinced from the first that organised sport would be beneficial to his patients, Guttmann insisted that it was incorporated into the rehabilitation programme at the Spinal Injuries Unit at Stoke Mandeville: 'The purpose of all remedial exercises in the period of re-conditioning of the paralysed is to develop new tricks for making muscles move parts of the body formerly moved by other muscles. These exercises should begin as soon as possible in the early stages of spinal paralysis while the patient is still confined to bed and should include sporting activities when he or she is able to get up and about in a wheelchair. The conclusion drawn by the famous physiologist Sir Charles Sherrington from his experimental work on animals – 'Each and every part of the animal is integrative' – can also be applied to man.

'Some handicapped individuals have taken up sport on their own initiative, sometimes against medical advice. They were by no means only those who had already been active in sport before they became handicapped ... This group includes some who were born with physical defects. In this respect, Lord Byron is a good example. Although handicapped by a congenital leg deformity, he took up rowing and swimming and excelled in boxing as a boy as well as

Thanks to Guttmann's determination, sports were no longer denied to the disabled, even internationally.

With a typically emphatic gesture Guttmann exhorts a disabled archer. Note the heavy, old-fashioned wheelchair.

The Wheelpast, a stirring opening to the 7th World Wheelchair Games, the Paralympics, July 1984, at Stoke Mandeville.

Terry Willett of the UK team wheels on to the six-lane track bearing the torch to ignite the specially designed bowl with the Olympic flame.

Fast, exciting and competitive: an international basket ball game in the packed stadium at the Ludwig Guttmann Sports Centre.

Two athletes at the International Games at Stoke Mandeville – *left* throwing the discus; *right* putting the shot – proving that with courage and training, excellence is within the grasp of disabled sportsmen and sportswomen.

Sir Ludwig and Lady Guttmann in their garden at High Wycombe with their eldest grand-daughter, Clare.

Joan Scruton, Ludwig Guttmann and Charlie Atkinson were so closely involved with every aspect of the Games at Stoke Mandeville that they were known as The Three Musketeers.

Meeting the competitors: HRH the Princess of Wales after opening the 1985 International Stoke Mandeville Games.

later in life. Other examples from the last century are two one-leg amputees, who, each having been provided with a wooden leg, competed with each other in a walking race during a sports festival at Newmarket Heath to the enthusiasm of the spectators.'

Joan Scruton believes there were special reasons why the concept of sport for the disabled was so readily accepted at the unit – by both patients and staff: 'The climate prevailing in those early days of the Spinal Injuries Unit was the best and perhaps the only way in which the sports movement for the paralysed could have developed into today's Olympic Games for the Paralysed. Our paralysed men and women at Stoke Mandeville became the banner-bearers of sport for other types of disabled. There was no question whether the patient *wanted* to undertake sport – like work, Dr Guttmann introduced it into the dynamic treatment programme of spinal cord injuries with the same importance as that of bladder and skin care. As a result, the majority of our patients came to *like* sport and to recognise not only its physical but also its social advantages.

'Most of the early patients at the unit, young men and women who had been severely wounded during the war, were mentally sound and had been accustomed to playing and watching sport all their lives. If a disabled person has already mastered a certain sport prior to his disability, he may utilise this particular sport in addition to conventional methods of physiotherapy to conquer his disability. He may even regain his former skill to such an extent as to be able to compete in high-class competitions with other disabled, and able-bodied, competitors.'

There are some sports – archery, dartchery (archery darts), bowling, snooker and table tennis among them – in which, with the necessary will and training, disabled players may compete with the able-bodied on equal terms. In a marathon, wheelchair athletes have a definite advantage over able-bodied competitors, since moving on wheels is mechanically more efficient than walking or running: in the London Marathon, wheelchair entries are given an official handicap. The first wheelchair marathon at Stoke Mandeville took place during the Paralympics of 1984, ninety-eight wheelchair athletes competing on a twenty-six mile course starting at Chalfont St Giles and finishing at the Ludwig Guttmann Sports Centre. The finishing time – by Rick Hanson of Canada – was 1 hour and 49.53 minutes, as opposed to the actual London Marathon over the same distance with the fastest recorded finishing time of 2 hours and 18 minutes.

It is also interesting to compare the percentage of both able-bodied and disabled athletes who still compete in international sports competitions after the age of thirty-five. A statistic compiled by *The Lancet* in 1975 showed that only seventeen per cent of competitors in the Olympic Games were over thirty-five, and in most cases they were competing in such events as sailing or sports which do not require great muscular effort. In contrast, a survey of 280 registered competitors in the 1974 National Stoke Mandeville Games for the Paralysed showed that 28.5% were over thirty-five. And at the International Stoke Mandeville Games held that same year, out of 538 competitors, 22.5% were over thirty-five. These disabled athletes took part in a wide spectrum of events – swimming, table tennis, weightlifting and even basketball. Guttmann concluded that 'This clearly shows that disabled sportsmen and women, even more than their able-bodied counterparts, are anxious to continue their competitive sporting activities into middle and later age.'

From the beginning, Guttmann struck a sympathetic response to the breakthrough he was seeking for the disabled. In British society, everyone, the physically handicapped as well as the able-bodied, relates to sport as an important aspect of leisure, so why should this 'passion for playful and recreative activity', as Guttmann described it, be denied a paraplegic?

Soon after the war, when Charlie Atkinson joined the staff at Stoke Mandeville Hospital straight from his Army service, he worked mainly with spinal patients, and quickly formed a close understanding and partnership with Guttmann, becoming a stalwart of the Games for the Paralysed movement. He stayed on at Stoke Mandeville until Guttmann's retirement in 1967; shortly afterwards they both moved literally a few hundred yards away to the sports centre.

'Dynamic wasn't the word for it,' Atkinson says of Guttmann, remembering his first years with the unit. 'He gave everything he had to the job at hand – and expected those of us who worked for him to do the same.' Recalling his introduction to archery: 'Poppa caught me and said "The English champion archer is coming down tomorrow to demonstrate archery to some of the patients. I want you to be there to take it all in, and afterwards I shall expect you to know all about it and be able to get the patients going." Just like that! This sudden call shook me at the time, although I was to realise later that it was to be the usual run of things . . . I smile now when I look back on that day, with our old wooden bows and wooden arrows and our short rounds and low scores, and compare them with today's equipment and scores which are equivalent to those of most able-bodied archers. Yet I feel that those early days and the tremendous effort put in by the first enthusiastic patients were really worthwhile . . . little did we realise we were starting a sport that was to prove ideal for paraplegics and one in which they could really lick the pants off most able-bodied teams.'

Guttmann, Joan Scruton and Charlie Atkinson were so closely involved with every aspect of the games at Stoke

Mandeville that they became known as The Three Musketeers. Atkinson found that sport, as part of the rehabilitation programme, was generally well accepted by the patients. 'We had one or two rascals who had to be pushed a bit, but they were all right once they got started!'

During the post-war period, with large numbers of spinal cord injured men and women still receiving hospital treatment, the cheering idea of 'sport' spread quickly from Stoke Mandeville to other spinal units. Anxious to establish contact between his own patients and others, Guttmann decided to arrange a sports festival for the disabled. On 28 July 1948, the first Stoke Mandeville Games for the Paralysed were held on the front lawns outside the hospital. The competitors were sixteen ex-members of the armed forces – fourteen men and two women.

Guttmann recognised the importance of this event: 'It was the first archery competition in the history of sport for the disabled. It was fought between a team from the Star and Garter Home in Richmond and one from Stoke Mandeville. The Star and Garter Home was the first winner of the Archery Shield Trophy, which I dedicated. Small as it was, it was a demonstration to the public that competitive sport is not the prerogative of the able-bodied, but that the severely disabled, even those with paraplegia, can become sportsmen and women in their own right.' And it was no coincidence that on the same day the legendary archery competition was taking place at Stoke Mandeville, King George VI was opening the post-war Olympics in London. Although it must have seemed highly unrealistic at the time, Guttmann's sights were already set on the Olympics for what he always thought of as *his* athletes.

Those first Stoke Mandeville Games, with their sixteen disabled archers, were pronounced a success, enjoyed by everyone involved, and that was all Guttmann needed. With

148

his energy, his drive, his ability to galvanise those around him into doing a job exactly the way he wanted, the Stoke Mandeville Games, he determined, would thereafter be held annually. For the thousands of handicapped people throughout the world, struggling to come to terms with severe disability and to restructure their lives, those first, simple Games marked a turning point. The idea of disabled men and women competing in their own sporting events at the highest level would, in time, be acceptable and even commonplace, largely through Guttmann's own belief and persistence.

Proof of the enthusiasm and interest the Games aroused came quickly. Each successive year the numbers of competitors, as well as spectators, increased. From the sixteen competitors from two hospitals in 1948, the following year there were sixty from five hospitals, and by 1951 one hundred and twenty-six competitors. In those early years, it was traditional for the Games to be opened with club-swinging demonstrations to musical accompaniment, given by patients in the unit who were still in the initial stages of rehabilitation. With the limited funds and facilities then available, it was all hands on deck. Eva Guttmann remembers that 'Dad roped me in at a pretty early age to pull arrows out of targets in the archery competition and pass round pints of beer at the end-of-Games party.' With trays of home-made cakes and sandwiches, friendships made and renewed from year to year, the Games took on the air of a family reunion.

Other sporting events were introduced – fencing, field and track, table tennis, snooker, weight-lifting, all played in wheelchairs. When the Ministry of Pensions built a specially heated indoor pool at Stoke, the first of its kind in any spinal centre in the world, swimming was added to the events and also, after an outdoor green was built through voluntary contributions, bowls. Understandably proud of the sports

149

movement he was building, Guttmann recalled that 'at the prize-giving ceremony in 1949, I was somewhat carried away by the success of the Games that year and I dared to express the hope that the time might come when this event would be truly international and the Stoke Mandeville Games would achieve world fame as the disabled men and women's equivalent of the Olympic Games.'

He did not have long to wait. The first of Guttmann's goals was realised in 1952. That year, a team of Dutch paraplegic war veterans from Aadenburg crossed the Channel to take on the British. Thus the *International* Stoke Mandeville Games were created'at only the fifth annual festival. A hundred and thirty competitors converged on Stoke Mandeville that year. In 1953 competitors came from other countries – Canada, Finland, France and the Netherlands. Word of the Games spread largely through the world-wide network of contacts Guttmann had made through the referral of other doctors, students and patients to the centre. The Spinal Injuries Centre was becoming recognised as one of the most progressive units of its kind in the world.

The disabled sports movement, organised and inspired at every step by Ludwig Guttmann, was gathering momentum. In September 1951 the unit had become the National Spinal Injuries Centre; support for Guttmann's work was now official. An International Stoke Mandeville Games Federation was formed and it was decided that the Games should take place at the end of July each year in memory of their foundation in the sports grounds of Stoke Mandeville Hospital. At that time, somewhat rashly, it was also mooted that whenever possible, and provided adequate arrangements could be made, the Games should be held every fourth year in the Olympic country. Ludwig Guttmann's second goal, the Paralympics, was in sight.

Behind the success of the Games lay sheer hard work and organisation; the sweat and discipline of training athletes; detailed arrangements for travel, food and accommodation. Looking back, Charlie Atkinson realised 'The organisation was hit or miss at first – like everything else in the Games. Gradually, we worked out a pattern and then it got easier ... We operated as a small unit, a family, led by Dr Guttmann. We knew what we'd set out to do. And *that* made the whole sports movement work.'

The size of an international team depended largely, as it still does, on the financing available. Some teams accept direct sponsorship; the first team from the United States competing in the Games in 1954 was sponsored by Pan American Airlines. A national team of eight competitors would be considered average today. Foreign or away teams must shoulder the expense of travel, uniform and equipment but the expenses of the Games themselves, including accommodation, are underwritten by the hosts. Host teams are much larger – perhaps between thirty and forty athletes, dependent upon the accommodation available.

An obvious difficulty in sport for the disabled is the question of classification. Skilled evaluation of a handicapped athlete's disabilities – as well as abilities – is crucial to the validity of any sporting event for the handicapped. It requires a professional who can also give guidance to the disabled sportsman or woman and the paramedical staff involved in his or her training, as Guttmann realised: 'The aim of this classification is to ensure fair play and to eliminate, as far as possible, injustices between participants in the same class and to give priority to the more severely disabled ... In cases of uncertainty, it is necessary for the classifying medical officer to watch a competitor's performance.' It sometimes happens that a competitor is given a different evaluation for different sporting events – say, swimming versus field

151

and track. For those athletes with very severe physical disabilities, a points system has been devised.

It was Guttmann's ideal that a physically handicapped man or woman, prepared for rigorous and disciplined training, should be accepted as athletes in their own right, just as the able-bodied. Therefore, rules for sporting events at the Stoke Mandeville Games followed, as closely as possible, the international rules for the same sports in competitions for the able-bodied. Modification of equipment, also, was kept to a minimum; in some cases, such as the javelin, the ladies' Olympic model was used instead of the men's.

'Over the years,' Guttmann explained in his *Textbook*, 'we have learnt a great deal about the degree to which these rules can be adapted to sport for the paralysed. Meetings of doctors, trainers and team leaders are held immediately after the Games every year. Every country taking part has the opportunity of airing comments and suggestions in the light of experience gained in the various events. These meetings have been of great importance in adapting and refining the rules of able-bodied sport to wheelchair sports.'

With his co-workers Joan Scruton and Charlie Atkinson, Guttmann compiled a *Handbook of Rules of the Stoke Mandeville Games*. Although this gradually became outdated as the Games grew and techniques were refined, it was accepted throughout the world as a basis by organisations concerned with sport for the paralysed.

As training methods improved, so disabled athletes gained confidence in their abilities. The standards of performance in all events improved steadily and, as Guttmann wrote with pride, 'almost every year, records are broken in one event or another'. This continues to be the case as the following comparisons prove:

Women – 100 metres Track	1981 – 21.50 sec
	1984 – 17.00 sec
Men – 100 metres Freestyle Swimming	1976 – 1:13.19
	1985 – 1:07.91
Men – 1500 metres Track	1980 – 4:22.90
	1985 – 3:58.50
Men – Discus	1974 – 37.80 metres
	1984 – 43.28 metres
Women – Shotput	1974 – 4.85 metres
	1984 – 7.19 metres

For many years, the Games continued to be held on the front lawns of the Stoke Mandeville Hospital and visiting teams were accommodated in the hospital. However, as the enterprise grew, the sports events were moved to a field behind the hospital and quite basic huts were constructed to house competitors.

A Paraplegic Sports Endowment Fund with its own committee and officers was set up, and grants were made by charitable supporters, such as the Royal Air Force Association, towards the building of this temporary accommodation. Each hut had about forty beds. Meals were eaten at tables running down the middle, the food brought on trolleys from the hospital kitchens. As the Games expanded, the fund increased its contributions as more facilities were added, and helped to underwrite the added cost of holding the Games.

Those who participated in the first years of the Stoke Mandeville Games look back on them with nostalgia. Professor Tricot led the first Belgian team in 1954, the third year of the International Games: 'This delegation had a symbolic European character, starring two Belgian nationals, a French boy and an Italian girl. Such was our first archery team.' He describes his initial impressions of the Games: 'This was the first time I was plunged into the dynamic and even intoxicating atmosphere of the Stoke Mandeville Games. Guttmann proclaimed his enthusiasm and his faith under the banner of the Games, saying that no greater contribution can be made to society by the paralysed than to help, through the medium of sport, to further friendship and understanding among nations.'

Guttmann's forceful persuasiveness in promoting the Games became legendary. Dr Bob Jackson, a recent President of the Stoke Mandeville International Games Federation, remembers his first casual meeting with Ludwig Guttmann ... Three hours later, he found himself having promised to bring a Canadian team – which did not then exist – to the next Games. And it was Guttmann, with his somewhat brash preference for going 'straight to the top', who invited Roger Bannister, fresh from the triumph of the first four-minute mile, to come to Stoke Mandeville to watch and encourage his own handicapped athletes.

An outstanding wheelchair athlete, Dick Thompson MBE, first met Guttmann in 1949 at the Stoke Mandeville Games: 'I was competing in archery and javelin throwing. Dr Guttmann was delighted that our contingent of four had travelled all the way from Hexham Spinal Unit in Northumberland at his invitation. I had broken my back in a climbing accident when I was seventeen and was paralysed from the chest down. This was a year later and I managed to win the javelin event, much to my amazement, not having thrown the javelin since I was at school. Poppa was delighted and said that I must go back to the Games next year. I had always been very keen on sport of all descriptions prior to my accident. From those Games he changed the whole course of my life. He gave me an interest in something I never thought I would ever do again. He gave me an added goal in my life to strive for.'

Thompson remained on good terms with Guttmann and, partly because of his athleticism, became 'something of his blue-eyed boy'. Guttmann even forgave a lapse when he drank too much one night before a competition – which he won anyhow. 'I never found out how he knew, but for years after that he would ask me if I still drank, and naturally I said "No" just to keep him happy!

'One year, I managed to throw a world record javelin throw. It was better than the able-bodied British javelin champion could do sitting in a wheelchair. It was typical of Poppa to organise a competition with the then British champion javelin thrower and the British champion shot putter, and put them in wheelchairs on equal terms with me. When he found out that I could beat their throws, he would have a great beam all over his face and I couldn't do a thing wrong in his eyes for a long time.'

Ludwig Guttmann sincerely believed that 'Sport is of even greater significance for the well-being of the severely disabled than the able-bodied'. Eventually, his philosophy was summed up in the symbol of the Olympics for the Paralysed – three intertwined wheels representing Friendship, Unity and Sportsmanship. As a doctor and a scientist who cared passionately about the needs of the disabled – and after fifty years of experience – Guttmann wrote that: 'Sport is invaluable in restoring the disabled person's physical fitness – his strength, co-ordination, speed and endurance. *In the contest with himself to improve his or her performance*, the physically handicapped person learns to overcome fatigue, a

155

predominant symptom in the early stages of physical rehabilitation, especially following fractures, amputations and paralysis. The initial cause of the handicap is of little importance.'

Guttmann also believed that sport in the life of a disabled
person was infinitely more important than merely a soph-
isticated form of physiotherapy: 'The great advantage of
sport over formal remedial exercise lies in its recreational
value ... by restoring that passion for playful activity – the
desire to experience joy and pleasure in life – so deeply
inherent in any human being. The aims of sport for the
disabled as well as the able-bodied are to develop mental
activity, self-confidence, self-discipline, a competitive spirit
and comradeship.'

Finally, Guttmann regarded sport as a prime means
through which the disabled person can be kept in contact
with the community as well as with his or her disabled peers.
Watching the hundreds of wheelchair athletes milling about
the Ludwig Guttmann Sports Stadium during the Games,
an onlooker is struck by the relaxed air of comradeship.
Confident and assured, men and women wheel themselves
deftly along paths, to and from the dormitories, in and out
of buildings where various sporting events are in progress.
Announcements, in many languages, come over the loudspeakers. Groups gather at the edge of the sports field to
chat, down a beer or eat a picnic lunch. Over the years,
friendships have been made between competitors, their trainers and their escorts. The spirit of the 'Festival' which
Ludwig Guttmann first envisaged in 1948 has remained:
an occasion for sportsmanship, meetings, reunions and an
exchange of news and ideas.

Mrs Gillian Matthew has been a competitor in the Games
over the past twenty years since she became paralysed after
a riding accident and found herself a patient of Guttmann's

at Stoke Mandeville. As part of her remedial therapy, she was introduced to swimming, table tennis and archery quite soon after her accident and from the beginning she did well: 'I had to swim twenty-five metres in my first Games and I was knocked out in the first round in table tennis. But I greatly enjoyed the competitions and meeting fellow paraplegics.' Speaking of her continuous participation in the Games she says that 'Poppa's sports movement has provided me with a form of safety valve. I have a busy life at home. My four children are now grown-up. My numerous outside activities all mean trying to keep up with able-bodied people. So I find my time at the Games, in the company of fellow disabled people, a complete relaxation – even though energetic. I return home better tempered and with the batteries recharged ... I am also grateful to Poppa because the sports are international and I have had several marvellous trips abroad, all great experiences that I would not otherwise have had.' This was exactly the response Guttmann hoped for, in his own patients and in others with similar disabilities.

In 1956, the International Olympic Committee awarded the Fearnley Cup to the organisation of the International Stoke Mandeville Games for 'outstanding achievement in the service of Olympic ideals'. It was a proud moment for Ludwig Guttmann. He had never forgotten that the first Stoke Mandeville Games had coincided with the opening of the post-war Olympics. And in 1960, for the first time, the International Stoke Mandeville Games were held abroad – in Rome, as Italy was the host country of the Olympics that year.

Guttmann described this milestone: 'Four hundred paralysed sportsmen and sportswomen representing the twenty-three countries joined in the competition held at the Olympic Stadium following the Olympic Games and under Olympic

Games conditions.' As these hundreds of handicapped athletes wheeled through the huge Olympic Stadium, someone
who was there remembers the atmosphere as 'moving – very
solemn'.

The Games were opened by the wife of the President of
the Italian Republic and caused a great deal of interest among
the public. When they were over, the late Pope John XXIII
gave a special audience in Vatican City to all the competitors
and their escorts. Speaking directly to the athletes, he said,
'You are the living demonstration of the marvels of the
virtue of energy. You have given a great example ... you
have shown what an energetic soul can achieve, in spite of
apparently insurmountable obstacles imposed by the body.'

The Pope then gave an audience to Father Leo Close from
Dublin, a former paraplegic patient of Guttmann's who had
been a competitor in the Games. 'He was ordained by special
permission of the Pope,' Guttmann wrote, 'and became the
first Catholic "priest on wheels".'

Professor Tricot who attended those games, noted that
on that occasion: 'The athletes were accommodated at the
Olympic Village. This was memorable chiefly for the efforts
the escorts had to make in pushing the chairs because of the
many steps of the building ...'

The second time the Games were held in the Olympic
country was in 1964, in Tokyo, the athletes competing in
the magnificent new Olympic Stadium immediately after the
Olympic Games. The Games were opened by the Crown
Prince and his wife, and members of the Imperial family
attended the Games during the week. Ever concerned with
furthering his message, it gave Dr Guttmann much satisfaction: 'The public took a great interest, as evidenced by
the attendance of more than a hundred thousand spectators.'
Undoubtedly these Games made a strong impact on the

Japanese: 'The Tokyo Games were outstanding in demonstrating the effect of sport of the disabled on society as a whole. The Japanese Government realised the capabilities of men and women in a wheelchair in the field of sport, and recognised the immense value of sport in the special rehabilitation of the severely disabled. Within six months, a factory had been set up for paraplegic and other severely disabled workers. There are at present several such factories in Japan, called Sun Industries, of which the late Dr Nakamura, an orthopaedic surgeon and former graduate of the Spinal Injuries Centre at Stoke Mandeville, was in charge.'

In 1968 it was not feasible to hold the Games in Mexico, the Olympic country. They were held instead in Israel, at Ramat Gan, near Tel Aviv. Almost twice as many competitors attended as in Tokyo – seven hundred and fifty, with three hundred and fifty escorts, represented twenty-nine countries. The Games were opened in the large University Stadium in Jerusalem by Yigal Allon, the deputy Prime Minister. Again, Guttmann noted with pride: 'The public followed the Games enthusiastically and a crowd of twenty-five thousand attended the opening ceremony. The final basketball match between the Israeli and American teams at Ramat Gan was attended by about five thousand people and a large crowd who could not get into the stadium had to be turned back ... General Dayan, who was the guest of honour, presented the trophies to the winning Israeli team.'

A recollection by Charlie Atkinson:

'My most memorable occasion? This is hard to say, as all our occasions have been memorable in their steps forward, but I think this is one of the outstanding.

'It was in the de Coubertin Stadium in Paris, on one of our first trips abroad. A French paraplegic team and ours were to play a match following a display and competition of top class able-bodied basketball players. To have to follow such a brilliant display filled us with misgivings as to the public reception of our match, so it was with mixed feelings that the French referee and I filed into the arena to start the game. There was a deathly hush during the first few minutes, and then a tremendous roar swelled the arena, as the crowd cheered on their French team, with the other referee and me being called all the usual names when we decided a foul against the local team!

'It was amazing; the crowd had forgotten that these people were in wheelchairs *and were just watching two teams of basketball players.* This was the highest compliment they could have been paid, and when we lined up for the National Anthems I looked up at Dr Guttmann in the box and could have sworn that behind those glasses his eyes were as moist as mine.'

Through his wide travels, often on behalf of the disabled sports movement, Guttmann became increasingly angered by the inaccessability of the majority of sports facilities and swimming pools everywhere *to the handicapped.* Even in newly built centres, he found a lack of ramps, toilets too narrow for a wheelchair, too many steps and small lifts. He concluded that although in recent years municipal authorities and architects had become more enlightened in building houses for the disabled, in general public sports and recreation units were built with only the able-bodied in mind.

Deeply involved in the organisation of the Games from their shaky beginnings, Joan Scruton also has very prosaic memories. 'We were,' she says, 'absolute martyrs to our English weather. Many a contest was carried out in drenching rain or bitter winds in order to get through our Games schedules. The wooden accommodation huts had to serve also as dining rooms, recreation rooms and as a refugee when the weather was bad. Even such uncomfortable conditions did nothing to dampen the ardour and enthusiasm of our disabled athletes – although I am not so sure about us able-bodied helpers ...' She also remembers the first spinal bus, donated by the British Legion – 'an old, converted London bus, noted for utility rather than comfort' – in which paraplegic archers were able to travel to matches with able-bodied clubs and other sporting events. Charlie Atkinson adds: 'The bus was painted blue and yellow, so I suppose people we passed on our journeys could be forgiven for standing open-mouthed watching us go by and thinking we were part of some circus. To load this "Pullman", you lowered the ramp, which was a terrific length, then took the patient and chair back a considerable distance. Starting at a gallop to the ramp, a superhuman effort pushed the chair up into the bus. If you were lucky and the ramp was not wet, you made it the first time, but often you made the halfway mark and then had to ease slowly down backwards and start again.'

For some years, as the Games at Stoke Mandeville had grown into a thriving international organisation, it had been Ludwig Guttmann's hope to create a permanent stadium which would act as a home base for disabled athletes of the world. The fields behind the hospital at Stoke Mandeville were becoming more and more inadequate for the yearly "Festivals", despite a purpose-built hostel for accommodation of competitors and their escorts. As Professor Tricot wrote: 'Guttmann went on dreaming or, more precisely, went on imagining ways to make his dreams come true.'

In 1967, on his retirement as Director of the National Spinal Injuries Centre, Guttmann decided that the time had come to act. The concept of the Stoke Mandeville Sports Stadium was born, and he set about making it a reality.

161

The original Games Fund had already become the Paraplegic Sports Endowment Fund, and it was with his colleagues on this committee that Guttmann first discussed the project. In many ways, the first hurdle – obtaining permission from the Ministry of Health to build a stadium on the sportsground of Stoke Mandeville Hospital – was the most difficult to overcome. Months of finicky negotiation ensued. 'Eventually,' Joan Scruton said, 'the magic day came when Dr Guttmann burst into the office brimming over with excitement that the PSEF had been granted a ninety-nine year lease of the group at a peppercorn rent.'

The next step was to raise £350,000, as a charity, from public subscription. That year, 1968, the Games were to be held in Israel so the committee had a little more than a year in which to raise the necessary funds and build the stadium in readiness for the Games the following year. As with everything in the sports for the paralysed movement, Ludwig Guttmann set about the project – the one which he said himself was 'closest to my heart' – in a strongly individualistic manner, as Joan Scruton recalled:

'A passionate non-swimmer, as Dr Guttmann used to describe himself, what more natural than that he should be invited to address a large congress of the Institute of Baths Management in Blackpool as guest speaker? It was there that he wandered around the Exhibition and visited the stand of a consulting engineer, which impressed him – as did the man himself. He immediately put to him a proposition: that he consider building us a stadium as a package deal. "It won't," he told the engineer, "make you a rich man. But you will have the satisfaction of having done something fine for humanity and this will stand you in good stead." It was typical Guttmann *chutzpah* and it worked.'

The deal was concluded and construction began. Unfortunately, the following autumn and winter were about the wettest on record, so work proceeded slowly. Guttmann visited the site so often – doggedly wading through oozing mud, chivvying everyone – that he became known to everyone involved as 'the Clerk of Works'. Joan Scruton:

'When time drew near for the completion date, which an unknowing observer would have judged to be at least a year away, Dr Guttmann learned that Her Majesty The Queen had graciously agreed to perform the opening ceremony. With only weeks left to finish the job, the engineer declared that it was not possible. "Let me talk to all the sub-contractors," said Dr Guttmann. And so he gathered them around him, and whatever he said to them did the trick, for the Stadium was ready in time – and was duly opened by The Queen during the Stoke Mandeville Games.'

But the saga was not yet finished: 'Just hours after Her Majesty left, the heavens opened and the approach to the stadium flooded, making access impossible. The engineer in charge was called from his bed in the early hours of the morning by an irate Ludwig Guttmann to come and put the matter right immediately.'

Guttmann's skills as a persuasive fund raiser were fully tested during that period. At one stage, serious lack of funds had threatened the work in progress on the stadium. Out of the blue, a telephone call from a friend of his daughter's who had also been a patient gave the good news that the British Paraplegic Sports Society had been given a substantial grant from a philanthropic trust fund of which he was a trustee. So the work continued, and the Stoke Mandeville Sports Stadium for the Paralysed and other Disabled, as it was first called, was opened free of debt.

Over the years, many facilities have been added to the original structure, such as the Lady Guttmann Indoor Bowls Centre, a four-hundred-metre all-weather track, a shooting range, table tennis and fencing halls. Ten different sports are now included in the International Stoke Mandeville Games programme: air weapons, archery, basketball, bowls, athletics, fencing, swimming, snooker, table tennis and weight-lifting.

The disabled sports movement, and the centre which would later take his name, increasingly monopolised Ludwig Guttmann's energies and his interest. After his retirement as Director of the National Spinal Injuries Centre in 1967, and a brief hiatus for research, he worked full-time as Director of the sports centre until the end of his life. A few handicapped athletes came to feel that Guttmann's insistence on excellence in *his* competitors, *his* Games was over-emphasised. Serious opposition to 'Poppa', on whatever grounds, was considered a breach of loyalty and not easily forgiven. But even those who were bruised by his powerful ego agree that without Ludwig Guttmann's drive – and passion – the disabled sports movement would not have achieved the world-wide acceptance it has today.

Nearing eighty, Guttmann began his last major venture – an Olympic village for the disabled, as part of the sports centre complex. Plans were already far advanced when he suffered his first major heart attack in September 1979. After his death in 1980, and despite huge problems, principally financial, his co-workers carried the project forward – guided, they believed, by what Ludwig Guttmann called 'the spirit of Stoke Mandeville', and they succeeded. Although he did not live to see it, the Olympic village, fully equipped and landscaped, awaited the first arrivals for the 1981 International Stoke Mandeville Games.

The Charter of Humanity

DURING LECTURES, Guttmann was frequently asked whether his own philosophy of the rehabilitation of severely disabled people could be summed up in one sentence. His standard, and highly characteristic, reply was: '*Yes. To transform a hopeless and helpless spinally paralysed individual into a tax-payer.*'

He would further explain to his astonished audience that 'although this might, on first hearing, sound rather materialistic, in fact it is the ultimate aim of rehabilitation. For such a disabled person can look anybody straight in the eye and say "I am as good as you, and perhaps even a little better, for to become a tax-payer in my condition, wheelchair-bound for life, I have first had to overcome one of the greatest tragedies in the human condition."'

The first Parliamentary Act in the United Kingdom which was fundamental in the social re-integration of the spinally paralysed and other severely disabled persons was the Disabled Persons (Employment) Act, which came into being in 1944. Guttmann described it as a 'charter of humanity which really legalised the modern concept of rehabilitation of severely disabled'.

This Act promoted training and facilities of employment to enable the disabled to obtain jobs in industry or to undertake work on their own account. It empowered the Ministry and Local Authorities to provide facilities for sheltered employment for those severely disabled persons who could not obtain employment in open industry in ordinary competitive conditions, but who were still capable of carrying out remunerative work as distinct from therapy. In addition, industrial rehabilitation units were set up in various parts of the country, and vocational training courses in nearly forty different trades in special training centres were started by voluntary organisations, with financial support from the Government.

Without doubt, this Act, and the changing social attitudes which it heralded, greatly facilitated the work on which Guttmann was embarked. Soon after the war, several other spinal units throughout the country were closed and the patients were transferred to Stoke Mandeville. The number of beds there rose to over a hundred, with the patients accommodated in six male and two female wards. With the growth of the unit at Stoke Mandeville, the facilities there gradually increased particularly in the departments of physiotherapy, occupational therapy, vocational training and sport. Also, a programme of regular school education for paralysed children was instituted.

In September 1951, Stoke Mandeville Hospital, with the exception of the Spinal Injuries Unit, was transferred to the National Health Service, and the unit came under the combined direct administration of the Ministry of Pensions and the Ministry of Health. It was then that the unit was officially recognised by both Ministries as the 'National' Spinal Injuries Centre. However, this status was not achieved without a good deal of tough talking behind the scenes. Despite strong opposition, Guttmann was absolutely determined that if he was to remain as Director, the Spinal Injuries Centre must have a *national* identity:

'There was a preliminary meeting of representatives of the Ministry of Pensions and the Ministry of Health, the Secretary of the Oxford Regional Hospital Board, and myself. Although most of these representatives ... were not in favour of the official grading of the centre as a *national* institution serving the greater community, I remained adamant. Only in this way could our pioneering treatment and research in this field of medicine be maintained. After the meeting, we gathered together for sherry in the office of the Deputy Superintendent, and I raised my glass to toast the National Spinal Injuries Centre! This was greeted by stunned surprise, followed by a roar of laughter. Shortly after, the Ministry of Health confirmed the *national* status of the centre.'

So Guttmann had his way. But in the process, he succeeded in antagonising a lot of people. He could never tolerate dissent. Even with his colleagues, on an equal footing, his relationships were often uneasy. His leadership was authoritarian – or at least domineering, as some might prefer to say – but he held to his vision and was willing and able to fight for it. He knew no other way. He was fair-minded enough to acknowledge later in life, the problems the 'National' Spinal Injuries Centre had posed for everyone involved at the time:

'For local administration as well as other departments of the hospital and the medical committee, it was unpalatable having a national unit admitting patients from other regions under the same administrative roof. There was even an attempt to change the name of Stoke Mandeville Hospital which, through the work of the spinal unit, had become well known. Naturally, I had to protest, and this idea was dropped ... But the firm stand I had to take in the interests of the future development of the centre, and above all for the sake of its patients, did not make me very popular!

'However, these difficulties gradually subsided and gave way to a better atmosphere all round, especially when it was realised that a Spinal Injuries Centre, even of this large size, was by no means a hindrance to the development of other specialised departments at Stoke Mandeville Hospital. On the contrary, other units made use of the special facilities afforded to the centre, such as the swimming pool and the increased physiotherapy staff. It can be said that Stoke Mandeville Hospital was one of the very few provincial hospitals in the country where there was never a shortage of physiotherapists, since so many physiotherapists from Britain and abroad came to Stoke Mandeville to be trained in our new approach and techniques. Physiotherapy schools of the London teaching hospitals sent their classes of students to the Centre routinely for lectures and demonstrations.'

Guttmann became a member of the Stoke Mandeville Committee and later also of the Aylesbury Hospitals Management Committee. He served for some years as Chairman of the Medical Advisory Committee. His relations with administrators in the Ministry of Health remained volatile, though he gamely admitted that many of them 'showed understanding and appreciation of the manifold technical and medical problems which were involved in the pioneer work for spinal cord sufferers at Stoke Mandeville'. One such administrator, with whom Guttmann had crossed swords many times, later wrote in the journal *Paraplegia*, on the occasion of Guttmann's seventieth birthday: 'I have been privileged to know and work with Ludwig for over twenty years. *No man with his drive and purpose could or should be a comfortable colleague for an administrator.'*

By the time the Spinal Injuries Centre became National, Guttmann's reputation was already established as a world leader in the treatment and rehabilitation of spinal cord-injured victims. During the years until his retirement from the Centre, he continued to work with undiminished vigour. Professor Whitterridge, in his biographical memoir for the Royal Society, commented with sad irony that 'few men have so exemplified the real virtues of the old Germany:

devotion to duty, systematic attention to detail and unflagging perseverence. If he had not had the tenacity to be in his wards every night at first until his orders were fully carried out, his work would have foundered.'

In 1947, Guttmann had been made a member of the Royal College of Physicians, exempted from taking the examinations in recognition of his previous work. This was a proud milestone even though, because of the Emergency Medical Services, he had already been practising clinical medicine in Britain for three years. As Director of the Spinal Injuries Unit at Stoke Mandeville, he also became consultant to many other spinal units and organisations in the country, among them The Star and Garter Home for ex-Servicemen in Richmond; Chaseley Home in Eastbourne; and The Duchess of Gloucester House in London, a Ministry of Labour hostel for paraplegics. He was also neurological consultant to the Oxford Regional Hospital Board. From 1952, he was consultant in Rehabilitation to the World Veterans Federation, and Founder-Chairman of the International Society for the Welfare of Cripples from 1953 for seven years. He became President of the International Stoke Mandeville Games Federation in 1959 and Founder-President of the British Sports Association for the Disabled in 1960.

Else and Ludwig had been among the first refugees from Germany to be naturalised after the war. In 1951, the Guttmanns had moved from Oxford to a large and attractive house in High Wycombe, still nearly an hour's drive from the hospital but a welcome change from the lengthy commuting Guttmann had by then endured for seven years.

Else continued her work for the Citizens Advice Bureau and for several Jewish women's organisations. Gardening became a new interest, and with talent and energy she transformed the big garden of their new home. It was she who managed the family's improved financial affairs, leaving her husband as free as possible of domestic considerations to pursue his career. Both children had adjusted satisfactorily after the dramatic flight from Germany, and had done well in their respective schools. Showing considerable intellectual gifts, Dennis Guttmann won a scholarship from The Dragon School to St Edward's, a public school in Oxford. Afterwards, with parental pride, his father enjoyed telling an amusing story about his school days: 'Dennis became a prefect and captained rowing. One day, before one of the annual school rowing races he came home rather dissatisfied with his crew, which consisted of the second son of Fisher, then Archbishop of Canterbury, and also the sons of seven other prominent churchmen. I tried to encourage him by saying: "Dennis, if Old and New Testaments are together in one boat, you *must* win." The next day, I was delighted to see his boat win by half a length . . .' Dennis was awarded an Exhibition at Magdalen College, Oxford, taking a First in physiology. He continued his medical studies at University College Hospital and did National Service in the RAF; later, he became a Consultant Physician at Peterborough.

After leaving Oxford High School for Girls, Eva went on to train as a physiotherapist in London. She married a young doctor, Frank Loeffler, now a Consultant Gynaecologist at St Mary's Hospital, Paddington.

For them, as for many Jewish and other refugee families, the end of the war brought tragic news of relatives who had remained in Germany. Else's sister, Irma, and her two children, a boy and a girl about the same ages as Eva and Dennis, were moved from Theresienstadt to Auschwitz in one of the last transports. All three perished. Irma's husband, a doctor, was kept on at Theresienstadt and survived. Ludwig's sister, Grete, and her husband also perished. News came, too, of Bernhard Guttmann. Interned in Theresienstadt, he had died there of malnutrition in 1942. He was seventy-three. The family had tried, right up to the last moment, to get him out of Germany to safety but he lacked the will: his wife had died in 1936 so he chose to stay on. Perhaps, even after his son and grandchildren had emigrated, he still could not bring himself to believe the imminent danger of his situation. Ironically, like so many Jewish men of his generation, he had served honourably in the German Army during the First World War. Thus was he 'rewarded'.

Despite the anguish and indignity they had suffered through the horrors of the Nazi regime, according to the Guttmann children both parents refused to look back in bitterness. They neither could, nor should, forget their past but they had built new lives for themselves, moved on. They had a growing family, a distinguished career, a pleasant home, friends, interests. They also retained many positive memories of their lives in Germany. Their own childhoods, and even the early years of adulthood before the Nazis came to power, had been stable and happy. Although their last frontier crossing at Colmar must have still been painfully vivid, both Ludwig and Else visited Germany quite soon after the war.

For the rest of his life, Guttmann would refer to this first return to Germany as his 'crossing of the Rubicon'. However, despite the emotional significance it held for him personally, the occasion turned out to be a curious, almost farcical, episode.

In 1947, Guttmann received a call from the Ministry of Health, asking if he had any knowledge of a new treatment for spinal cord injuries being carried out in Kassel, in Germany, which was reputed to be dramatically successful. Of course he had not. Would he be willing to go to Germany and investigate? With his expertise in the field and his German background, he was the obvious choice. Guttmann hesitated, but believing it to be in the country's interest and also professionally curious, he agreed to go.

He was flown to Kassel in a military plane. On his arrival, he was shattered to see the extent of the bomb damage, far greater than he could have imagined. The whole area, he said, was 'a shambles'. In some streets there was barely a house still standing but the clinic, on a hill outside the town, was undamaged. Guttmann immediately enquired of the doctor in charge the secret of his reputed new treatment. After the briefest explanation, both men burst out laughing, realising the mistake at once. Press reports had muddled the German word *Kur*, spa, with the English *cure*. The magic treatment was no more than a course of atropine injections already well known to neurologists and thoroughly investigated.

The mystery solved, Guttmann prepared to return to England immediately, but the German doctor was most welcoming and asked him to stay and examine the patients. Afterwards, he asked his wife to go into the town to a restaurant that was still standing and buy a bottle of special Franconia wine. The two doctors reminisced together about their respective medical trainings in pre-war Germany.

In such a way, Ludwig Guttmann's 'Rubicon' was passed. In 1954, he gave his first lecture in Germany, in Hamburg, since leaving the country fifteen years before. As a German who was also a Jew and who had therefore been persecuted and forced into exile, Guttmann found, not surprisingly, that the Germans he met on what was after all his native soil, tended to treat him with some embarrassment: 'I would have been shocked if I had been told by Germans "*I was never a Nazi.*" When I went to Hamburg, and on subsequent visits, people came up to me and said: "Look here, can you forgive me? I was a Nazi." This I found acceptable.' It was a source of grim satisfaction that in 1957, as part of the Restitution Law, his degrees and qualifications, which had been voided by the Nazis, were fully reinstated.

Else Guttmann took her daughter back to Freiburg in the early 1950s. Despite the searing memories the visit must have evoked in her mother, Eva remembers it as a pleasant stay. Else was able to show her daughter the old haunts in the Black Forest where she had spent the carefree years of her youth, when the political evils ahead – and emigration from the country she loved – were unimaginable.

Also in the 1950s, Guttmann was able to revisit Breslau, then renamed Wrozlaw, after a conference on rehabilitation held near Warsaw organised by a former pupil of his, Professor Marian Weiss. Guttmann wrote movingly of this bitter-sweet return to the town where he had lived and worked, where his children had been born and where he had established the career which was to become synonymous with the words Stoke Mandeville.

'Practically nothing was left standing of the whole vast southern part of the city, which had been almost wiped out when it was defended to the last. It was a nightmare to me to find no familiar landmark amongst the waste of dust and rubble, with here and there an isolated building standing like a tombstone. Guided by the old water tower, which resembles a magnified old Bavarian stone beermug in shape, I succeeded in finding my way to the Jewish Hospital.

'What memories came flooding back as I was gripped by nostalgia and a sense of tragedy and sadness! Although this hospital was still standing, it was partly destroyed, and there were completely blank areas in its neighbourhood where once familiar buildings and streets had stood, including Gutenberg Street nearby where we had lived. The Wenzel Hancke Krankenhaus, where I had started my career as a neurologist and neurosurgeon, was also partly destroyed. Foerster's neurological department had been transformed into offices and lecture rooms, including its operating theatre, which had become a library. Alas – his Rockefeller Research Institute had been turned into a hostel for students engaged in the study of Catering! *Tempora mutantur!*

'Many years afterwards, I had a second opportunity to revisit Breslau, which had been beautifully rebuilt by the Polish authorities but which was just as unfamiliar to me. However, the former Jewish Hospital had been restored to a hospital (for railway workers). Seeing the main entrance to the administration block reminded me vividly of that ominous action of the Gestapo on 10 November 1938.'

It was at that time, also, that Guttmann was able to visit his mother's grave, a profoundly emotional experience. Thanks to the diligent efforts of his Polish friends, it had at last been found amid all the destruction. He had been devoted to her in life – her first child and only son – and he revered her memory, speaking and writing of her with deep affection. Since her death he had become a citizen of another country; he had worked indefatigably; he had achieved much. Now, getting on in years, he was returning to his roots.

'The lady from the Department of Health in Wrozlaw was waiting for me at the gates and guided me down a pathway through the wilderness of that former cemetery to the grave. Although the tombstone had been destroyed by vandals, her grave was renovated and decorated with lighted candles and flowers planted by local boy scouts. At the head of the grave was a plaque with the inscription "Dorothea Guttmann, mother of Professor Ludwig Guttmann, distinguished pioneer in the rehabilitation of the disabled." I was deeply moved . . .'

*   *   *

Under Guttmann's dynamic and highly visible leadership, the unit had quickly attracted the attention of medical bodies throughout the world. Doctors, students and physiotherapists found their way to Stoke Mandeville to study the innovative scientific work and practical management of patients by Guttmann and his staff. Some came to visit quite briefly, others actually worked there for short periods. One such doctor was a Frenchman called Paul Dollfus. A victim of polio in childhood, he was himself confined to a wheelchair. His comments on the unit, which he wrote for the coming-of-age issue of *The Cord*, are particularly revealing of the standards, and the atmosphere, he found there as a temporary member of the staff:

To describe a stay of four and a half years at Stoke Mandeville seems to be an arduous task, so many impressions ... and just a few lines to describe them!

Working in a wheelchair seems something so normal that I was still astonished to find colleagues walking along those long, long corridors which could be, at times, so congested with 'wheelchair traffic' you could think you were motoring along one of London's main arteries at six o'clock in the evening! It is a good thing wheelchairs have no exhaust!

Working as a doctor in a very busy hospital can be tough. Working at Stoke Mandeville was tougher, in a wheelchair hardly more. At least I was at the same level as the patients, most of them, but I would say my worst enemies were the famous 'Packs'. These were parcels of pillows raising the patient so high in the bed that catheterisation of the bladder was like planting a flag on top of a mountain!

Working in a wheelchair can give a real advantage over able-bodied colleagues. Finding out that one is part of 'them' immediately opens many doors to the hearts and understanding of patients, who little by little become your friends.

It is true that sometimes, not wearing the traditional white coat – one has to 'scrub up' so often – some new patients thought I was pulling their leg when I hurriedly came along and asked them to lie on their bed for examination . . .

Working on the staff of Stoke Mandeville was quite an experience, not only for an able-bodied person but also for any disabled. The famous Stoke Mandeville 'air', which is not mentioned in any touristic or climatic brochure, is certainly invigorating (with the help of sometimes a few blood transfusions). You always leave a little of your heart and spirit in a place where you have learnt so much, not only on the scientific aspect of paraplegia but also, which is at least as important, on the human side.

Dr Dollfus later became Director of a spinal centre in Mulhouse, France.

Inevitably, young doctors such as Dollfus took away something of that spirit, and many of the techniques, which they found at Stoke Mandeville, incorporating them into units where they worked both in Britain and abroad. In later years, Guttmann saw spinal units named after him set up in such diverse parts of the world as Heidelberg, India and the Instituto Guttmann in Barcelona. He visited Israel in 1972 to advise the government in planning a spinal injuries centre, and laid the foundation stone of what would eight years later become the Sir Ludwig Guttmann Institute at Tel Hashomer Hospital. These tributes gave him deep satisfaction as 'honours which I have very much appreciated'. They were, in fact, tangible proof that his mission had succeeded.

As a disciplined scientist who was anxious to record his life's work for the purposes of teaching and posterity, Guttmann persevered with his writing: 'All my experiences gained with the new concept of treatment and rehabilitation of spinal cord sufferers have culminated in *The Textbook on Spinal Cord Injuries: Comprehensive Management and Research.*' This was first published in 1973 and was followed by *A Textbook of Sport For the Disabled*. Both books are still considered 'Bibles'.

Every year, beginning in 1952, scientific meetings were held during the International Stoke Mandeville Games, vitally important in giving surgeons, physicians and paramedics the opportunity to exchange views and experiences. Believing that these quite informal seminars should be made official, in 1961 Guttmann founded the International Medical Society of Paraplegia, becoming the first President and retiring in 1969. In 1963, the Society established its own journal, *Paraplegia*, as 'an international forum for easy exchange of ideas for all concerned with the welfare of our spinally paralysed fellow men and women'. Today it is a highly respected publication, appearing every two months and uniting the society's widely scattered members. Guttmann was the first editor, succeeded by Dr Phillip Harris of Edinburgh.

In 1965, the National Spinal Injuries Centre celebrated the twenty-first anniversary of its founding. To mark the occasion, and in the presence of staff and patients both past and present, Ludwig Guttmann's portrait was unveiled. The artist, Sir James Gunn, had died before it was quite finished, but the likeness to its subject is well and truly caught. It shows a portly man, getting on in years, in a white coat and with a decidedly humorous glint in the eyes. Warm, direct, a bit testy, 'Poppa' had the look of a man you would want on your side.

Today, the portrait hangs in the boardroom of the Ludwig Guttmann Sports Centre for the Disabled at Stoke Mandeville, home of the aspect of his work closest to his heart. 'If I ever did one good thing in my medical career,' he wrote with pride, 'it was to introduce sport into the rehabilitation of spinal cord sufferers and other severely disabled men and women.'

At the age of eighty, Guttmann was asked by an interviewer: 'When does a refugee stop being a refugee?' His answer, definite but quite without rancour, was '*Never!*' All the same, during his years of intensive work at Stoke Mandeville – and while he was simultaneously developing the Games for the Paralysed – he became a much honoured member of Britain's medical establishment. He was made a member of the Royal College of Surgeons in 1961, the same year in which he was given an honorary degree of Doctor of Surgery at Durham University. Similar degrees were accorded him at Trinity College, Dublin in 1969 and at Liverpool University in 1971. He was awarded an OBE in 1950, just three years after acquiring British citizenship, the CBE in 1960 – and he was knighted in 1966. During one of the investitures the family attended with him at Buckingham Palace, Eva distinctly remembers the band playing 'I'm gonna wash that man right out of my hair ...' The jaunty tune and catchy words seemed exactly to fit her father's irrepressible personality.

In addition to his tireless efforts to promote the Games, for which he displayed a natural flair and showmanship, Sir Ludwig also travelled constantly in his capacity as Director of the Spinal Injuries Unit. From 1947 he visited more than thirty countries in Europe, North and South America, Australia and the Far East to advise on the treatment and rehabilitation of paraplegia. Governments, universities, societies and other institutions invited him to lecture, to present papers and to inspect their facilities. He refused to mince his words when he found standards unacceptable. During one of his visits to Australia, an eyewitness reported that he 'almost caused a riot in one hospital ... a complete pantomime erupted when Sir Ludwig caught sight of a paraplegic patient wasting away in one of the wards. The language flowed and the gestures were eloquent ... and quickly resulted in changed treatment.' He was only a little more circumspect when he found medical situations with which he profoundly disagreed in spinal units in Britain.

Even a cursory look at some of the honours bestowed on Guttmann shows the considerable extent of his international reputation. Apart from his connection with many organisations, world-wide, through the International Stoke Mandeville Games, they include visiting professorships at Columbia University and Duke University in America; a street, Dr Guttmann Laan, named after him at Doorn in Holland; honorary membership of La Societé Française de Neurologie; Japan's Order of the Rising Sun; and membership of the highly esteemed Athenaeum Club in London. His opinion was much sought after, particularly in the United States, in accident insurance cases. In this regard, he never moved from his rigidly held belief that in almost all cases of severe spinal cord injury, surgical intervention was mistaken 'meddling' – or useless. His willingness to appear as an expert witness was a source of controversy among neurological colleagues in Britain.

In 1967, Sir Ludwig retired as Director of the National Spinal Injuries Centre, though for two more years he continued his research work there. In 1969, moving his office only a few hundred yards away, he became full-time Director of the BPSS at the new Ludwig Guttmann Sports Stadium for the Disabled. When he left the centre, Stoke Mandeville stood for the most enlightened care and rehabilitation of spinal cord injured men and women anywhere in the world. He had done his job; achieved more than even *he* could have imagined back in those first war-time days. In 'retirement' he was continuing to do the work to which he had devoted his life. And he had always admitted that the development of the Games had been the aspect of his work which had given him the deepest personal satisfaction.

The success of his philosophy had been proved, incontrovertibly, by Guttmann and his staff at Stoke Mandeville. The following statistics, compiled in 1963, of 3000 patients admitted to the unit from its opening on 1 February 1944, show how fundamentally both the life expectancy, *and the quality of life*, had changed for spinal cord injured victims who were treated there. 2012 patients were considered ready for employment; 84.5% of them were already employed in various jobs and professions, just over half of those being in full-time employment. The mortality rate, which had been as high as 80% in the First World War, was cut dramatically.

In addition to his work for the BPSS at the Sports Stadium, Sir Ludwig continued to give lectures all over the world and he was away on one of his lecture tours of the United States when Else suffered a tragic accident. Returning from a family gathering in Glasgow in 1972, she picked up her car at London Airport and set out to drive home to High Wycombe. On the way, she was involved in a serious crash. Although the gravity of her injuries was not immediately apparent, she went into a coma. Returning at once, Sir Ludwig had her transferred from the Radcliffe Hospital in Oxford where she had been taken – to the National Spinal Injuries Centre. Though she lived on for more than a year – an agonising time for her family – she died without regaining consciousness.

Until the accident, she had led a busy life, involved with her family, her home and garden and her community activities. At seventy, she was still an enthusiastic skier. Else and

Ludwig Guttmann had met and become friends when he was a young medical student and she still a schoolgirl. They had endured many ups and downs in more than forty years of married life; had known tragedy, made difficult decisions and experienced reversals as well as success. It is likely that her husband's brilliant career owed more to Else Guttmann's unstinting support, her strength and her domestic competence than he ever realised. Normal family life is rarely compatible with outstanding achievement.

During Else's illness, Sir Ludwig had moved from the large house in High Wycombe to a modern bungalow in Aylesbury. He lived alone, excellently cared for by a part-time housekeeper and friends from the stadium. Many of his colleagues from his earliest days at Stoke Mandeville, including Joan Scruton who was now his assistant director at the BPSS, lived close by. Eva drove down from London to visit him often.

He went on working just as hard, lecturing, planning. The Paralympics had grown into a huge international organisation involving thousands of disabled sportsmen and women, their doctors, coaches and therapists. He still enjoyed travelling and later in 1972 he went off to lecture in Colombia S.A. The following year he visited Malaysia at the invitation of the Malaysian Government, to advise on the planning of a national spinal injuries unit. In 1974 he was named consultant to UNESCO International Congress on Sport and Physical Education in Moscow.

In 1976 Sir Ludwig received the highest accolade of all, Fellowship of the Royal Society. Those closest to him believe that of all his many awards and citations, this honour, bestowed upon him by the peers he admired, gave him the most pride.

Apart from his work, which still consumed him, he had many other satisfactions which brought him contentment.

Both his son and his son-in-law had established distinguished medical careers, Dennis as a Consultant Physician in Peterborough, Frank Loeffler as a Consultant in Gynaecology and Obstetrics in London, and as editor of *The Journal of Gynaecology*. He took pleasure in the progress of his five lively and intelligent grandchildren. One grandson, Mark Loeffler, began medical studies at the London Hospital and has since qualified.

An interview taped for the archives of the Imperial War Museum, recorded in Guttmann's eightieth year, shows that his mental powers were as alert as ever. The German accent is unmistakeable. The voice is a bit hoarse, but he speaks emphatically. He deals sharply with questions he considers trivial or unclear. His reminiscences of his early medical career and the life of his family in Germany under the Nazi regime bring modern history to life with astonishing clarity. Occasionally, his voice shakes with outrage. He does not give the impression of bitterness.

His eightieth birthday party, held in July 1979 at a London hotel, was an exuberant affair. Prince Charles was guest of honour and both he and Sir Ludwig made witty speeches. All Sir Ludwig's family, including some members from the United States, attended. Also present were many of the 'family' acquired down the years at Stoke Mandeville, old patients and friends. A leavening of show business personalities whom Sir Ludwig had come to know from his work and his fund-raising added to the sparkle – Jimmy Saville, Les Dawson, Ernie Wise. The Prince of Wales was heard to remark, as he led Margot Fonteyn to the dance floor, that it was too bad she had to end her career in this manner . . . a happy and glowing evening, to be remembered.

Less than three months later, the day after he had given a lecture at the Royal Society of Medicine, Sir Ludwig suffered a coronary thrombosis. Fast medical attention saved his life. When he had left hospital and was well enough, he went to Peterborough to stay with his son Dennis and daughter-in-law, Helga. Dennis Guttmann recalls, with some amazement, that this was the first time in his life he had ever seen his father relax. An elderly man, recovering from severe illness, he needed the comfort of a caring home, and his two small grandchildren, Hannah and Jonathan, provided his entertainment. In pre-war Germany, the family had employed a live-in servant and he had had little to do with his own two children at that age. He saw, possibly with some regret, how different was his son's relationship with his children. From Dennis's earliest memories, his father had been ceaselessly busy, totally involved in the Jewish Hospital, the centre and the Games, always planning, travelling, intent on the next goal. Now, father and son had the leisure – albeit enforced on Sir Ludwig's part – to get to know each other and to enjoy each other's company. They did.

Sir Ludwig appeared to make a good recovery and on Christmas Eve that year was able to put in an appearance at least at the traditional staff party at the Stadium in Stoke Mandeville. There was, however, a most distressing situation to be faced, and which could not be withheld from him. The centre was seriously threatened, although the Games, a separate organisation, were not.

For some time, renovation and modernisation of the National Spinal Injuries Centre had been urgently required. Parts of the centre were, literally, falling to bits. Rather than allocate urgently needed funds, the Ministry of Health had taken the decision to phase out the centre – and had begun closing down some of the wards. Although family and friends worried about the effect this calamitous situation might have on Sir Ludwig's uncertain health, he responded characteristically by firing off outraged letters in whatever direction he thought might help, and assuring both the staff and patients at the centre of his total support. At the same time he helped to launch the Stoke Mandeville Appeal which, under the brilliant direction of Jimmy Saville, eventually succeeded in a way that would have made Sir Ludwig extremely proud. But it was principally the outcry of the patients, some of whom chained themselves to beds and doors, that won over public opinion, and forced the Ministry of Health to reconsider. The new National Spinal Injuries Centre at Stoke Mandeville, built at a cost of approximately £10 million raised by public subscription, was opened by HRH The Prince of Wales in July 1983. In April 1985 the Department of Health announced a £10.5 million reconstruction of Stoke Mandeville Hospital.

In the spring of 1980, Sir Ludwig was invited by friends to visit Egypt. By then, he was feeling very much better and had returned to work part-time, and so, accompanied by Joan Scruton, he went. It was, she said, 'a magical time'. He was enthralled by everything he saw, appearing as he rarely did, very tranquil. They arrived back at London Airport on 18 March. His daughter, Eva, wrote four years afterwards: 'He spoke to me on the evening of his return. "I've had a wonderful holiday," he said. "Rode on a camel and went on a boat trip on the Nile. Marvellous fun. Wouldn't have missed it for anything." That night he died.'

Tributes came from many whose lives had been touched – with hope, with knowledge, with kindness and sometimes in anger – by this remarkable man. But the tribute which would have undoubtedly pleased him most was spoken, fittingly, by his son. Dennis Guttmann opened the International Stoke Mandeville Games in the summer of 1980, four months after Sir Ludwig's death:

'I looked out at the ranks of disabled sportsmen and women from all over the world in front of me on the

184

field at Stoke Mandeville, the stadium to one side ...
and I did away with most of my prepared speech ... I
thought – and I said – "You are his memorial." '

ACKNOWLEDGEMENTS

Foremost, the family of Ludwig Guttmann – Dennis, Eva, Frank, Helga and Clare – for their sympathetic co-operation and for making available to me Sir Ludwig's unfinished autobiography and tapes recorded for the Imperial War Museum.

Miss Joan Scruton, MBE, Director General of the British Paraplegic Sports Society, for her help and kindness. Also her secretary, Miss Kate Lambrechts; Professor David Whitteridge; Dr Jack Walsh; Dr Phillip Harris; Mr Charlie Atkinson; Mr Dudley Sutton.

Dr H. L. Frankel, consultant to the Spinal Injuries Centre, for his courtesy in inviting me to the Centre's fortieth anniversary party – on 1 February 1984 – where I met some of the first patients and the staff who cared for them.

Mrs Bertha Guttmann, a friend not a relative of the Guttmanns in Breslau, who talked to me about their life in that lovely city before the war; Mrs Meg Weston-Smith, a schoolfriend of Eva's, who contributed her recollections of the Guttmann family in Oxford.

Dr Frank Loeffler and Mr Charles Goodman, for their photographs of the opening of the Paralympics at Stoke Mandeville.

My editors, Roger Schlesinger and Gill Gibbins, who recognised the intrinsic worth of this story – and helped me to record it.

34 Montagu Square
London W1

April 1986

INDEX